Family Consecration
to Jesus through Mary

Other books by Donna-Marie Cooper O'Boyle
from Sophia Institute Press:

By Dawn's Early Light
Prayers and Meditations for Catholic Military Wives

Advent with Our Lady of Fatima

Our Lady's Message
to Three Shepherd Children and the World

Donna-Marie Cooper O'Boyle

Family Consecration to Jesus through Mary

33 Days of Preparation
with Saint Louis Marie de Montfort

SOPHIA INSTITUTE PRESS
Manchester, New Hampshire

Sophia Institute Press
Box 5284, Manchester, NH 03108
1-800-888-9344

www.SophiaInstitute.com

Sophia Institute Press® is a registered trademark of Sophia Institute.

ISBN 978-1-64413-263-0

Library of Congress cataloging-in-publication data has been applied for.

First printing

With great love for my children:
Justin, Chaldea, Jessica, Joseph, and Mary-Catherine,
and my grandchildren: Shepherd and Leo

As well, with great affection to
the Blessed Virgin Mary, our Queen, our Star of the Sea

Contents

Part 2
Obtaining Knowledge of Yourself

Part 3
Obtaining Knowledge of the Blessed Virgin

Part 4
Obtaining Knowledge of Jesus Christ

Appendices

Preface

How do we get to Heaven? How do we help our children and grandchildren to get there? We know without doubt that our salvation comes through Jesus. Many of the saints, however, have preached the need to get close to the Blessed Virgin Mary so that she can bring us close to her Son, Jesus. Saint Louis Marie de Montfort has said that devotion to Mary is the surest, shortest, and most perfect way to approach Jesus.[1]

Let's step back a couple of thousand years to a small town called Cana in Galilee, where Jesus, Mary, and the first disciples were guests at a Jewish wedding feast. These Jewish feasts were steeped

---

[1] Saint Louis de Montfort, *True Devotion to Mary: With Preparation for Total Consecration* (N.p.: Montfort Missionaries, 2002), no. 55, http://www.montfort.org/content/uploads/pdf/PDF_EN_26_1.pdf.

in tradition and rituals and generally lasted for about seven days while an exorbitant banquet of food and wine was continuously lavished upon guests throughout the festivities.

Imagine how shameful it would be for the bride and groom should they run out of wine for their honored guests. That's exactly what happened at that wedding feast. Jesus' Mother, Mary, did something about it. Being attentive to the needs of the bride and groom, not wanting them to be embarrassed, she made their needs known to her Son.

"They have no wine" (John 2:3). Jesus told His Mother that the time had not yet come for Him to begin His public ministry. What did Mary do? The holy Mother succinctly instructed the wine stewards, "Do whatever he tells you" (John 2:5). And Jesus provided an abundance of the best wine ever!

Saint John the Evangelist, writing his Gospel after a long life and inspired by the Holy Spirit, made sure that we would know that Mary's presence was significant. Through his writings, we recognize that the Blessed Mother's presence was worthy of attention in the carrying out of Jesus' first public miracle. Mary was always involved in her Son's ministry—she was there from the very beginning to the very end. As well, she is still working hard from Heaven!

The Blessed Mother always leads us to her Son. She desires that all of mankind would "do whatever he tells you." She would like us all to be safely in Heaven one day. It was Jesus who gifted us with His Mother as He was dying on the Cross for our salvation. "Behold your mother" (John 19:27), He told His disciple John. Mary then became the Mother of the Church.

Doctor of the Church Saint Alphonsus Maria Liguori put it this way:

> In His eagerness to show you mercy, God has given His Son
> as your Advocate. And then to make your confidence even

stronger, He has given you another Advocate, who obtains through her prayers whatever she asks. Go to Mary, and you will see salvation.[2]

The United States Conference of Catholic Bishops has stated:

Mary embraces God's will and freely chooses to cooperate with God's grace, thereby fulfilling a crucial role in God's plan of salvation. Throughout the centuries, the Church has turned to the Blessed Virgin in order to come closer to Christ. Many forms of piety toward the Mother of God developed that help bring us closer to her Son. In these devotions to Mary, "while the Mother is honored, the Son, through whom all things have their being and in whom it has pleased the Father that all fullness should dwell, is rightly known, loved and glorified and ... all His commands are observed." The Church honors her as the Mother of God, looks to her as a model of perfect discipleship, and asks for her prayers to God on our behalf.[3]

Since the Annunciation, and throughout salvation history, the Blessed Mother has always cooperated with the Holy Spirit and worked alongside her Son. She is our intercessor and our advocate. She is our Mother! Saint John Paul II stated, "Mary intensely and mysteriously unites her life with Christ's sorrowful mission: she was to become her Son's faithful coworker for the salvation of the human race." Listening to and following the requests of our Mother

---

[2] Saint Alphonsus Liguori, *The Glories of Mary: Explanation of the Hail Holy Queen*, rev. ed. (Totowa, NJ: Catholic Book Publishing, 1981), chap. 6, sect. 3.

[3] United States Conference of Catholic Bishops (USCCB), "Mary," USCCB, website, http://www.usccb.org/prayer-and-worship/prayers-and-devotions/mary/index.cfm.

in Heaven will lead us directly to the Sacred Heart of Our Lord and Savior, Jesus Christ.

Mary is to be highly praised. Saint Bonaventure tells us that "all the angels in heaven unceasingly call out to her: 'Holy, holy, holy Mary, Virgin Mother of God.' They greet her countless times each day with the angelic greeting, 'Hail, Mary,' while prostrating themselves before her, begging her as a favour to honour them with one of her requests."[4] They long to serve her. We can strive to imitate the holy angels.

The revelations of the saints have taught us that God desires a greater devotion to His Blessed Mother. One saint in particular, Saint Louis Marie Grignon de Montfort, exuberantly proclaimed, "God wishes that His holy Mother should now be more known, more loved, more honored, than ever she has been." And he added, "And this will no doubt come to pass, if the predestinate will enter, by the grace and light of the Holy Ghost, into the interior and particular practice which I will discover to them."[5]

This eighteenth-century French Roman Catholic priest and confessor was on fire with love and devotion to the Mother of God. He worked tirelessly to teach and preach. Clement XI made him a missionary apostolic in France so that he could fight against Jansenism, which was prevalent at that time. Saint Louis de Montfort's prophetic writings and preaching had a remarkable influence on the Catholic Church and continue to do so.

Saint Louis believed that Jesus is not known enough because Mary is not known enough. The unstoppable saint had preached that when "the Blessed Virgin Mary, who brought Him [Jesus] into

---

[4] Quoted in *Treatise on True Devotion to the Blessed Virgin*, no. 8, https://www.ewtn.com/catholicism/library/treatise-on-true-devotion-to-the-blessed-virgin-6064.

[5] Saint Louis de Montfort, *True Devotion*, no. 55.

the world for the first time," is more known, she will make "His second advent full of splendor."[6] Let's keep in mind that Saint John Paul II was deeply impacted by the writings of Saint Louis de Montfort. At one point, Saint John Paul II questioned his own Marian devotion, being concerned that his deep devotion to Mary might overtake his worship of the Lord Jesus Christ. The pope read Saint Louis's *True Devotion to the Blessed Virgin*, however, and his fears evaporated, because he realized that his Marian devotion would only help his Christological devotion. Ever since learning from Saint Louis, Saint John Paul II kept his Marian devotion central to his interior life and his spiritual theology.

Pope Pius XII proclaimed in his encyclical *Ad Caeli Reganim*:

> The Blessed Virgin possessed, after Christ, not only the highest degree of excellence and perfection, but also a share in that influence by which He, her Son and our Redeemer, is rightly said to reign over the minds and wills of men. For if through His Humanity the divine Word performs miracles and gives graces, if He uses His Sacraments and Saints as instruments for the salvation of men, why should He not make use of the role and work of His most holy Mother in imparting to us the fruits of redemption?"[7]

Back to those two questions I asked earlier, "How do we get to heaven?" and "How do we help our children and grandchildren to get there?" Well, I must tell you that I am deeply touched by Saint Faustina's words. In her *Diary*, she explained one of her visions, in

---

6 Ibid., no. 158.
7 Pope Pius XII, encyclical *Ad Caeli Reganim* (October 11, 1954), no. 42, http://www.vatican.va/content/pius-xii/en/encyclicals/documents/hf_p-xii_enc_11101954_ad-caeli-reginam.html.

which she encountered a crowd of children about five to eleven years of age. They cried out to her, "Defend us from evil." Saint Faustina then saw the Lord Jesus, who was distressed and told her, "You are to defend them from evil." Saint Faustina said that from that moment she prayed for the children. She added, "But I feel that prayer alone is not enough."[8]

Helping children to be consecrated to Jesus through Mary will surely help to "defend them from evil" by greatly aiding their souls. It will be more than simply praying for them. Remember, Saint Faustina expressed that she believed that "prayer alone is not enough." Your children's consecrations will surely please Jesus and Mary too. It will certainly help pave the way to Heaven.

There is no better time than right now to seize the opportunity and help your family to consecrate their lives to Jesus through Mary. Your total consecration will be a perfect renewal of your baptismal vows, with Mary at your side and through her loving hands and Immaculate Heart.

Throughout this book, your family will be guided with powerful teachings from Saint Louis de Montfort on Jesus, on true devotion to Mary, and on consecrating yourselves to Jesus through Mary. In addition, some powerful Marian saints will also enlighten, illuminate, and guide your family through thirty-three days of preparation, culminating in your very blessed Family Marian Consecration together. Indeed, your Family Consecration will help not only the souls of your family, but also those whom you come in contact with.

I highly encourage you and your family to renew your consecration each year. It will help to build up your "armor."

---

8 Saint Maria Faustina Kowalska, *Diary: Divine Mercy in My Soul* (Stockbridge, MA: Marian Press, 2014), no. 765.

May God bless you and your family, now and forever! May our dear glorious Mother in Heaven stand by you throughout your preparation and consecration and every day of your life!

Yours in Jesus, Mary, and Joseph,
Donna-Marie Cooper O'Boyle
September 12, 2019
Most Holy Name of Mary

How to Use This Book

This book will thoroughly prepare your family (ages seven and up) to consecrate their lives to Jesus through Mary. After going through your thirty-three days of preparation together as a family you will make your consecration together as a family. What a blessed day that will be!

First, decide when you will start your preparation. You may start at any time, but it is meaningful to make your consecration on a Marian feast day and start your preparation thirty-three days before it. To help you choose a feast day and determine when you should start your preparation, a chart is included following this section.

Next, choose a time of day that works best for your family to get to the "meat and potatoes" of the teachings each day; this might be when you're gathered together at the breakfast table or at the dinner table or before bedtime. It's a good idea to be flexible with the needs of your family, which means that your time to gather for your "preparation" might change on a daily basis. A parent or grandparent can plan on a fifteen- to twenty-minute commitment each day in going over the teachings and praying the prayers. It is up to you to decide how much additional effort you'd like to invest in your preparation. Suggestions will be provided about how you might continue the theme throughout the day.

For instance, you can open this book in the morning and pray the day's short morning prayer, alone or together. If not in the morning, later, you can gather the family to spend your time on the lesson (the nitty-gritty of the consecration preparation).

If desired, in the evening, you can pick up the book again for the short evening prayer. However, you will decide if you would like to add those extra times of prayer during your thirty-three-day preparation for family Marian consecration.

Particular spiritual exercises recommended by Saint Louis Marie de Montfort will be noted in each section of the book. A suggested family activity is provided at the end of each part of the preparation. A family crowning of the Blessed Mother is recommended at the time of your family consecration.

This book is not meant to apply pressure on you or your family. With anything worthwhile and any kind of devotional, however, it's good to keep in mind that a commitment is required in order for you to learn and to grow in holiness. Saint Louis de Montfort prescribed a thirty-three-day preparation period.

Because I want to stay true to Saint Louis de Montfort's teachings, I have shared in this book his recommendations and prescribed readings. I have attempted to coherently present the seventeenth-century teachings and writings that St. Louis promotes from *The Imitation of Christ*, by Thomas à Kempis (1380–1471), for your ease in understanding. I have used a more modern translation that retains the flavor of the original English translation.

Keep in mind that when teaching the Faith to your children, it is essential to keep a loving and gentle spirit and avoid strict regimentation. We want to instill a deep love for Jesus and Mary in your children, and not inadvertently cause your children to become fearful.

God knows that family life is very busy! If you miss a day of preparation, just pick up where you left off on the following day and add that day's teaching as well. There's no need to feel stressed or that you have failed in some way. God loves you and is on your side!

It is my hope and prayer that you and your family will come to know Jesus and Mary in a much deeper way through your family consecration to Jesus through Mary. I hope you will decide to renew your consecration each year (on the same feast day or on a different one).

Consecration Dates

Start Date of Preparation	Marian Feast	Consecration Date
January 9	Our Lady of Lourdes	February 11
February 20 (February 21 in leap years)	Annunciation	March 25
April 10	Our Lady of Fatima	May 13
April 28	Visitation	May 31
Date Varies	Immaculate Heart of Mary	Saturday after Corpus Christi
June 13	Our Lady of Mount Carmel	July 16
July 13	Assumption	August 15
July 20	Queenship of Mary	August 22
August 6	Nativity of Mary	September 8
August 10	Most Holy Name of Mary	September 12

Start Date of Preparation	Marian Feast	Consecration Date
August 13	Our Lady of Sorrows	September 15
September 4	Our Lady of the Rosary	October 7
October 19	Presentation of Mary	November 21
November 5	Immaculate Conception	December 8
November 9	Our Lady of Guadalupe	December 12
November 29	Mother of God	January 1
December 31	Presentation of the Lord	February 2

Family Consecration
to Jesus through Mary

Part 1

Emptying Yourself of the Spirit of the World

Twelve-Day Initial Period

Saint Louis de Montfort heartily believed that it was necessary to take twelve days of preparation in order to empty oneself of the "spirit of the world" as the beginning of a preparation for consecration to Jesus through Mary.

While you attempt to "empty yourself" of the spirit of the world, try your best to stay away from worldly things and unnecessary technology. Put your whole heart into it.

This period's spiritual exercises: pray, examine your conscience, practice renouncement, mortification, and purity of heart; this purity is the indispensable condition for contemplating God in Heaven, for seeing Him on earth, and for knowing Him by the light of faith.

Day 1

Be Countercultural

If then we are establishing sound devotion to our
Blessed Lady, it is only in order to establish devotion
to our Lord more perfectly, by providing a smooth but
certain way of reaching Jesus Christ. If devotion to our
Lady distracted us from our Lord, we would have to
reject it as an illusion of the devil. But this is far from
being the case. As I have already shown and will show
again later on, this devotion is necessary, simply and
solely because it is a way of reaching Jesus perfectly,
loving him tenderly, and serving him faithfully.[9]

—Saint Louis de Montfort

---

[9] *True Devotion to Mary*, no. 11.

Family Consecration to Jesus through Mary

Morning

Raise your heart and mind to God. Put yourself in His presence. Pray your Morning Offering and the following prayer:

Dear Lord Jesus, I place my trust in You. Please guide me this day as I begin my preparation for consecration. Dear Mother Mary, please intercede for me for the graces that I need most today. Help me to turn away from the world's allurements. I entrust my day to you. Dear Saint Joseph, please teach me to walk in your ways of holiness. Amen.

Teaching for Parents

Today, you begin your preparation, which, according to Saint Louis de Montfort, is the beginning of emptying yourself of the spirit of the world. Saint Louis prescribed reading the Beatitudes and reading about salt and light and about the law and the prophets. Take time to read and ponder.

The Beatitudes

When Jesus saw the crowds, he went up the mountain; and after he sat down, his disciples came to him. Then he began to speak, and taught them, saying:

Blessed are the poor in spirit, for theirs is the kingdom of heaven.

Blessed are those who mourn, for they will be comforted.

Blessed are the meek, for they will inherit the earth.

Blessed are those who hunger and thirst for righteousness, for they will be filled.

Blessed are the merciful, for they will receive mercy.

Blessed are the pure in heart, for they will see God.

Blessed are the peacemakers, for they will be called children of God.

Blessed are those who are persecuted for righteousness' sake, for theirs is the kingdom of heaven.

Blessed are you when people revile you and persecute you and utter all kinds of evil against you falsely on my account. Rejoice and be glad, for your reward is great in heaven, for in the same way they persecuted the prophets who were before you. (Matt. 5:1–11)

Salt and Light

You are the salt of the earth; but if salt has lost its taste, how can its saltiness be restored? It is no longer good for anything, but is thrown out and trampled under foot.

You are the light of the world. A city built on a hill cannot be hid. No one after lighting a lamp puts it under the bushel basket, but on the lampstand, and it gives light to all in the house. In the same way, let your light shine before others, so that they may see your good works and give glory to your Father in heaven. (Matt. 5:13–16)

The Law and the Prophets

Do not think that I have come to abolish the law or the prophets; I have come not to abolish but to fulfill. For truly I tell you, until heaven and earth pass away, not one letter, not one stroke of a letter, will pass from the law until all is accomplished. Therefore, whoever breaks one of the least of these commandments, and teaches others to do the same, will be called least in the kingdom of heaven; but whoever does them and teaches them will be called great in the kingdom of heaven. For I tell you, unless your righteousness exceeds that of the scribes and Pharisees, you will never enter the kingdom of heaven. (Matt. 5:17–20)

Teaching for Children

Read the Scripture verses above to your children. Choose a few (or all) of the Beatitudes and explain them to the children. But first, ask them a couple of questions.

For instance:

+ Who are the pure in heart?
+ How do we become pure?

Then explain why the pure in heart will see God. Do this with at least two or three beatitudes and build upon that with your teaching. Listen carefully to your children's responses and encourage them to share from their hearts. You can ask them why the Beatitudes sound contradictory. In other words, they are not like the teachings of the world. You can impress upon them that when Jesus taught the Beatitudes, He was sharing about the life of a true Christian—someone who is selfless, loving, and merciful. Encourage your children to strive to be more like Jesus—selfless and full of love and mercy.

Talk about "Salt and Light." Ask a few questions:

+ Why are we called to be salt and light?
+ Why shouldn't we hide our light?
+ In what ways might we hide our light?
+ What are three good ways to let our lights shine?

Discuss: "The Law and the Prophets." Ask your children:

+ Why did God make rules for us to follow?
+ Is He strict?
+ Or, is it because He loves us?
+ Should we always follow God's commandments?
+ What is one way that you follow God's laws?

Carry Out

Throughout this day, try your best today to carry out at least one interior practice of devotion to the Blessed Mother and one exterior practice. For suggestions, see the appendix "Interior and Exterior Practices" in this book. Help your children to decide what they should do. As well, ask them to try their best to be more like Jesus today. Keep in mind that Saint Louis de Montfort preached that devotion to Our Lady is "a means of finding Jesus Christ perfectly, of loving Him tenderly, of serving Him faithfully."[10]

Family Prayer

Saint Louis de Montfort prescribed certain prayers to pray during this twelve-day period. While gathered together, turn to the appendix "Prayers for Consecration Preparation" and pray the Veni Creator Spiritus, the Ave Maris Stella, and the Magnificat.

Find time today to pray the holy Rosary.

Evening

As evening falls, take a few moments to ponder the events of your day. Ask forgiveness for your shortcomings and for grace to do a better job tomorrow. Call upon the saints and holy angels to be with you and your family this evening. Remember that you are earnestly preparing your hearts for your consecration and desiring to empty yourself of the spirit of the world. Strive to focus on holiness and spend less time on secular activities.

Be sure to instill a healthy dose of peace and happiness in your family's hearts at bedtime. Get into the habit of blessing the family

---

[10] Saint Louis de Montfort, *True Devotion*, no. 62.

with holy water before going to bed. End the evening with inspiring and uplifting words or stories, lots of warm hugs, and good-night kisses. Let everyone know that they are loved!

Mary, My Mother

Dearest Mary, my Mother, I entrust my entire day to you—all that was good and all of the areas in which I might have failed. Kindly, make my efforts more holy and pleasing to your Son. Please help me each day as I prepare to consecrate my life to your Son, Jesus, through your most tender and loving hands and Immaculate Heart. *Hail Mary . . .*

Day 2

Be Holy and Humble

The Immaculate alone has from God the promise
of victory over Satan. She seeks souls that will
consecrate themselves entirely to her, that will
become in her hands forceful instruments for the
defeat of Satan and the spread of God's kingdom.[11]

—Saint Maximilian Kolbe

---

[11] Jill Haak Adels, *The Wisdom of the Saints: An Anthology* (Oxford: Oxford University Press, 1987), 18.

Family Consecration to Jesus through Mary

Morning

Raise your heart and mind to God. Put yourself in His presence. Pray your Morning Offering and the following prayer:

Dear Lord Jesus, thank You for the gift and blessing of a new day. Dear Mother Mary, I give you this day—help me to use it well in serving God, my family, and my neighbor. Dear Saint Joseph, be with me as I move through today. Amen.

Teaching for Parents

Yesterday, you studied the Beatitudes and were encouraged to lead a countercultural life and strive for holiness. You also discussed being salt and light to this needy world and talked about keeping the Commandments.

Today, again you are reminded of your call to holiness, but are given an extra challenge—to be holy, yes, but to do things in secret! You will read Scripture passages about being perfect like your heavenly Father; that you should not parade your good deeds around but should pray in secret; and that you need to be forgiving.

Begin by reading this short verse: "Be perfect, therefore, as your heavenly Father is perfect" (Matt. 5:48). A tall order? Yes, but our Lord calls us to it. With God's grace, we can surely work toward this goal.

Next, read and ponder the following:

Concerning Almsgiving

Beware of practicing your piety before others in order to be seen by them; for then you have no reward from your

Father in heaven. So whenever you give alms, do not sound a trumpet before you, as the hypocrites do in the synagogues and in the streets, so that they may be praised by others. Truly I tell you, they have received their reward. But when you give alms, do not let your left hand know what your right hand is doing, so that your alms may be done in secret; and your Father who sees in secret will reward you. (Matt. 6:1–4)

Concerning Prayer

And whenever you pray, do not be like the hypocrites; for they love to stand and pray in the synagogues and at the street corners, so that they may be seen by others. Truly I tell you, they have received their reward. But whenever you pray, go into your room and shut the door and pray to your Father who is in secret; and your Father who sees in secret will reward you.

When you are praying, do not heap up empty phrases as the Gentiles do; for they think that they will be heard because of their many words. Do not be like them, for your Father knows what you need before you ask him.

Pray then in this way:
Our Father in heaven,
Hallowed be your name.
Your kingdom come.
Your will be done,
On earth as it is in heaven.
Give us this day our daily bread.
And forgive us our debts,
As we also have forgiven our debtors.
And do not bring us to the time of trial,
But rescue us from the evil one.

Family Consecration to Jesus through Mary

For if you forgive others their trespasses, your heavenly Father will also forgive you; but if you do not forgive others, neither will your Father forgive your trespasses. (Matt. 6:5–15)

Teaching for Children

Talk to your children about almsgiving. Let them know that, as Christians, we are called to help others in some way—we give alms with objects, deeds, prayers, and words. Give some examples to your children. Explain the meaning of the verse "Whenever you give alms, do not sound a trumpet before you, as the hypocrites do in the synagogues and in the streets, so that they may be praised by others." Let them know that sometimes when we give to others, some people might see our good actions, and that is okay. We are not trying to draw attention to them. In those instances, God will use our kind deeds, works, and prayers as a beautiful example to help others and to inspire them to do the same.

At other times, our works of mercy will be done in secret. Only God and the receiver of the gift will know. God will be pleased and will reward you for both kinds of almsgiving. The important thing to impress upon your children is that we should not do our good deeds to be noticed.

It is the same for praying. We pray from our hearts because of our love for God. We don't parade our prayers around to make us look holy. When we pray sincerely, however, we will always be a good example to anyone who might observe us.

With regard to praying the Our Father and forgiving, teach your children that we should always want to forgive others their trespasses. Sometimes it is very difficult to do so if we still feel hurt by someone. But God calls us to rise above it. He wants us to ask Him for the grace to forgive and to push beyond our comfort zones and forgive others. It is the sure way to peace!

Carry Out

Throughout this day, try your best to be mindful of the day's teachings. Consider ways that you can give alms sometime soon. This might be through deed, word, or prayer. Help your children to decide how they can give alms. As well, seek to be perfect "as your heavenly Father is perfect." Pray the Our Father very slowly together so that your children can really tune in to how God wants us to forgive.

Family Prayer

While gathered today, to aid you in your preparation and your emptying yourselves of the spirit of the world, pray the prayers recommended by Saint Louis de Montfort: the Veni Creator Spiritus, the Ave Maris Stella, and the Magnificat. They are found in the appendix "Prayers for Consecration Preparation."

Find time today to pray the holy Rosary.

Evening

In the evenings, during prayer before bed, try to get into the habit of spending a few moments pondering the events of your day. How did you do? Ask forgiveness for your shortcomings and for grace to do a better job tomorrow. Your little ones will need some help with this. Work hard on striving for holiness. You will all reap the benefits!

Always end on a happy note! Finish the evening with inspiring and uplifting words or stories, lots of warm hugs, and good-night kisses. Let everyone know that they are loved!

Mary, My Mother

Dearest Mary, my Mother, thank you for being with me this day as I have tried to walk forward in faith during my preparation to make my consecration to your Son, Jesus, through your loving hands and Immaculate Heart. Please gather up all of my efforts today, as poor as they may be, and transform them into a fragrant bouquet for your dear Son. *Hail Mary . . .*

Day 3

Try to Be Like God

My dearest daughter, keep in mind that all the
living are born destined for death, but ignorant of
the time allowed them; this they know for certain,
however, that the term of life is short, that eternity
is without end, and that in this life only they can
harvest what will yield life or death eternal.[12]

—The Blessed Mother to Venerable Mary of Agreda

[12] Venerable Mary of Agreda, *The Mystical City of God: A Popular
Abridgment*, trans. Fiscar Marison (Charlotte, NC: TAN Books,
2012), chap. 8.

Family Consecration to Jesus through Mary

Morning

Raise your heart and mind to God. Put yourself in His presence. Pray your Morning Offering and the following prayer:

Dear Lord Jesus, thank You for caring for me through the night and gifting me with a new day. I pray to use the present moments of this day well. Dear Mother Mary, help me to be attentive to serving lovingly my family and my neighbor. I entrust my day to your care. Saint Joseph, I need your help today. Guide me, please. Amen.

Teaching for Parents

Today, you begin your third day of your preparation, which, according to Saint Louis de Montfort, is a process of emptying yourself of the spirit of the world. Saint Louis prescribes reading Matthew 7:1–14. These readings help to prepare your hearts, minds, and souls.

Judging Others

Do not judge, so that you may not be judged. For with the judgment you make you will be judged, and the measure you give will be the measure you get. Why do you see the speck in your neighbor's eye, but do not notice the log in your own eye? Or how can you say to your neighbor, "Let me take the speck out of your eye," while the log is in your own eye? You hypocrite, first take the log out of your own eye, and then you will see clearly to take the speck out of your neighbor's eye. (Matt. 7:1–5)

Profaning the Holy

Do not give what is holy to dogs; and do not throw your pearls before swine, or they will trample them under foot and turn and maul you. (Matt. 7:6)

Ask, Search, Knock

Ask, and it will be given you; search, and you will find; knock, and the door will be opened for you. For everyone who asks receives, and everyone who searches finds, and for everyone who knocks, the door will be opened. Is there anyone among you who, if your child asks for bread, will give a stone? Or if the child asks for a fish, will give a snake? If you then, who are evil, know how to give good gifts to your children, how much more will your Father in heaven give good things to those who ask him! (Matt. 7:7–11)

The Golden Rule

In everything do to others as you would have them do to you; for this is the law and the prophets. (Matt. 7:12)

The Narrow Gate

Enter through the narrow gate; for the gate is wide and the road is easy that leads to destruction, and there are many who take it. For the gate is narrow and the road is hard that leads to life, and there are few who find it. (Matt. 7:13–14)

Teaching for Children

Read today's Scripture verses to your children. These are foundational teachings that we carry through life. Try not to rush through them. Plan to take a few extra minutes to go over these teachings today.

Starting with "Judging Others," explain that we should not judge others, for we cannot see their hearts and souls, and we do not know their circumstances or their intentions. Only God can judge. Let your children know that there is a difference between judging and discerning. For instance, when we have a gut feeling about someone or when we know from a person's errant behavior (or the bad fruits of his behavior) that he is not someone we should imitate—that is a discernment. Discerning does not mean judging a person's soul. It's important to be attentive and to observe; by doing so, we can protect our hearts and souls from dangerous exposure by staying away from bad influences.

On the other hand, if we jump to conclusions and condemn a person because of his words or actions, then we are judging that person. Instead, we should pray for the person. We should want them to make it to Heaven one day. Let your children know what it means to see the "speck" of error in someone while at the same time having a "log" in our own "eye."

Explain to your children that we each have faults and that every day we are to work out our salvation throughout our daily routine—our experiences and encounters. We are steady works in progress. We need to try hard, and we should pray to improve. The goal is to become like God! Scripture tells us, "Be imitators of God, as beloved children" (Eph. 5:1).

"Profaning the Holy": Let your children know that not everyone believes in God and not everyone appreciates hearing about God. We can, however, pray for such people to get to Heaven one day. We can also pray for ourselves, that we may understand God better.

Saint Benedict composed this prayer, which you can pray together:

Gracious and Holy Father, please give me: intellect to understand you, reason to discern you, diligence to seek you, wisdom to find you, a spirit to know you, a heart to meditate upon you, ears to hear you, eyes to see you, a tongue to proclaim you, a way of life pleasing to you, patience to wait for you and perseverance to look for you. Grant me a perfect end, your holy presence, a blessed resurrection, and life everlasting. Amen.

"Ask, Search, Knock": Explain to your children that we should always seek God. We should never tire of asking Him for anything in prayer and, in asking, should recognize that God knows what is best for our souls. We can't have everything we ask for, or else we might not make it to Heaven! We need to trust God, who will always take care of us in the best possible way.

"The Golden Rule": Simply, we should always be good to others. Using examples in the family, tell your children that they need to treat their parents, siblings, and friends in the same way that they wish to be treated by them—always with kindness.

"The Narrow Gate": Tell your children that Scripture teaches us that the world is full of allurements that can take us away from God and our reward of Heaven. That is the "wide" gate. The "gate" that opens to Heaven is narrow. It is also a difficult journey at times, but the great reward will be Heaven. Impress upon your children that, by following God's laws, the Ten Commandments, and by loving Him and our neighbor, we are forging our way to Heaven.

Carry Out

In the verse that began our reflection today the Blessed Virgin Mary emphasized that we have only today. We are unsure of the future. Mary expressed, "The term of life is short." She said, "Eternity is without end." As well, Mary said it is in this life only that we "can harvest what will yield life or death eternal." Keeping her sobering, yet extremely helpful message in mind today, encourage your family to use their day wisely—to be good to others, to be prayerful, and to be mindful of the teachings you have learned today. Remember, it is easy to be good to those who are good to us and not so easy to return a blessing for a "curse." In other words, the challenge lies in those times when we are treated unjustly. How will we respond? We need to pray for the grace to do God's will.

Ask your children to carry out a secret act of kindness for someone in your family today and to pray extra prayers for that person (perhaps three Hail Marys).

Family Prayer

While gathered today, to aid you in your preparation and your emptying yourselves of the spirit of the world, pray the prayers recommended by Saint Louis de Montfort: the Veni Creator Spiritus, the Ave Maris Stella, and the Magnificat. They are found in the appendix "Prayers for Consecration Preparation."

Find time today to pray the holy Rosary.

Evening

As evening falls, encourage your family members to take a few moments to reflect on the day and ask forgiveness for any shortcomings and for the blessing of a new day tomorrow to strive for holiness once again. Help your little ones with this.

Earnestly strive to prepare your heart for your consecration during this time. Try hard to empty yourself of the spirit of the world. Work at focusing on holiness and spend less time on the secular.

End the evening with inspiring and uplifting words or stories, lots of warm hugs, and good-night kisses. Let everyone know that they are loved!

Mary, My Mother

Dearest Mary, my Mother, thank you for being with me and helping me to move forward in faith during this preparation to make my consecration to your Son, Jesus, through your loving hands and Immaculate Heart. Please grant to me the many graces that I need. I am confident that with your help, I will make my way closer to your Son's Sacred Heart. I fully entrust the fruits of this day to you. *Hail Mary* . . .

Day 4

Improve with Prayer

In this dangerous pilgrimage of life God has
ordained, that no one shall know for certain,
whether he is worthy (Eccles. 9:1) of His love
or hate; for if he uses his reason rightly, this
uncertainty will urge him to seek with all his
powers the friendship of that same Lord.[13]

—The Blessed Mother to Venerable Mary of Agreda

---

[13] *Mystical City of God*, chap. 8.

Family Consecration to Jesus through Mary

Morning

Raise your heart and mind to God. Put yourself in His presence. Pray your Morning Offering and the following prayer:

Dear Lord Jesus, the morning dawns, and I come before you in thanksgiving for this new day. Please open my heart to hear Your word so that I may serve You and all in my midst. Dear Mother Mary, show me how to serve your Son, Jesus. I humbly ask for your graces. I entrust my day to you. Dear Saint Joseph, help me not to worry about the past, but prayerfully to move forward. Amen.

Teaching for Parents

Today, as you begin your fourth day of your emptying yourselves of the spirit of the world, Saint Louis de Montfort prescribes reading *The Imitation of Christ*, which is said to have been written by Thomas à Kempis between 1418 and 1427 for the purpose of aiding readers to model themselves after Jesus Christ, who said, "I am the way and the truth and the life. No one comes to the Father except through me" (John 14:6). You will become more familiar with *The Imitation of Christ* as you move through this book.[14]

Man Has No Good in Himself and Can Glory in Nothing

Lord, what is man that You are mindful of him, or the son of man that You visit him? What has man deserved that

---

[14] The devotional classic *The Imitation of Christ* has been translated into more than fifty languages (by 1779 there were already 1,800 editions)!

You should give him Your grace? What cause have I, Lord, to complain if You desert me, or what objection can I have if You do not do what I ask? This I may think and say in all truth: "Lord, I am nothing, of myself I have nothing that is good; I am lacking in all things, and I am ever tending toward nothing. And unless I have Your help and am inwardly strengthened by You, I become quite lukewarm and lax."

But You, Lord, are always the same. You remain forever, always good, just, and holy; doing all things rightly, justly, and holily, disposing them wisely. I, however, who am more ready to go backward than forward, do not remain always in one state, for I change with the seasons. Yet my condition quickly improves when it pleases You and when You reach forth Your helping hand. For You alone, without human aid, can help me and strengthen me so greatly that my heart shall no more change but be converted and rest solely in You.[15]

Teaching for Children

Thomas à Kempis's words might go straight over your children's heads. Rather than read the selection to them, teach today's lesson in a simple fashion. Ask your children some questions and help them with their answers.

- *Why do you think God made you?* God made us because He loves us and wants us to be happy with Him forever. He made us to live forever. After our life on earth, we will live forever in eternity. For this reason, we work hard each

---

[15] Thomas à Kempis, *The Imitation of Christ*, bk. 3, chaps. 7, 40 (Milwaukee: Bruce, 1949), available at Christian Classics Ethereal Library, http://www.documentacatholicaomnia.eu/03d/1380-1471,_Kempis._Thomas,_The_Imitation_Of_Christ,_EN.pdf.

day to be good in this life, to love God and our neighbor, and help those in need.

- *Is God always good?* God is always good and will always help us. We should pray for His help every day.
- *Are we always good?* No, we are not. Sometimes we make bad choices. Sometimes we hurt others.
- *What can we do when we make mistakes and hurt others and God?* We can confess our sins and try harder next time. Asking God for the graces to make us stronger will help us to make better decisions. Encourage your children to make good choices in choosing whose examples they will imitate. You might talk about Saint Dismas, the "Good Thief" (Luke 23:40–41) whose crime we don't know. We do know, however, that he hung on a cross right next to Jesus. Before he died, he recognized his guilt, repented, and asked help from Jesus as the other thief ridiculed Him. Jesus forgave him and said, "Amen, I say to you, today you will be with me in Paradise." Your children will learn the power of repentance and forgiveness. After a life of sin, Saint Dismas was granted paradise. Now is a good time to tell your children a short story about a saint's mistake and how he or she improved. You can also mention Saint Matthew, the tax collector, and how he changed his ways after Jesus' invitation "Follow me" (Matthew 9:9–13). At that time, some were scandalized that Jesus dined with sinners and tax collectors. And we see that Jesus' invitation (to Saint Matthew and ourselves) and our acceptance, as well as turning from sin, makes us new people, transformed—true followers of our Lord. You might also mention Saint Augustine if your children or grandchildren are old enough to understand the kind of

sinful life that he led before converting. Or explain to them how the saints (or even yourselves or people you know at church) spend time together to guide, console, correct, and uplift one another. We need one another on this sometimes arduous pilgrimage through life. Allow time for a discussion.

Carry Out

In our reflection today, we see that our "condition quickly improves when it pleases" God and when He strengthen us so that our "heart shall no more change but be converted and rest solely in" Him. Spend time today considering the great loving hand of God and the need to stay close to Him and not give in to temptations and the allurements of the world. Strive to entrust your life to God more wholeheartedly.

Help your family to plan heartfelt works of mercy that you all can carry out soon. Jot down a few ideas when together at the dinner table. Do your best to put them into action soon. As well, don't forget about the dying and the souls in Purgatory. Keep them in your prayers.

Family Prayer

While gathered today, to aid you in your preparation and your emptying yourselves of the spirit of the world, pray the prayers recommended by Saint Louis de Montfort: the Veni Creator Spiritus, the Ave Maris Stella, and the Magnificat. They are found in the appendix "Prayers for Consecration Preparation."

Find time today to pray the holy Rosary.

Family Consecration to Jesus through Mary

Evening

Take a few moments to ponder the day and ask forgiveness for any shortcomings and the blessing of a new day tomorrow to strive for holiness once again. Remember that you ought to be earnestly preparing your heart for your consecration during this period of time, and you should pray to desire to empty yourself of the spirit of the world. Strive to focus on holiness and spend less time on the secular during this distinctive time of preparation.

Always tuck the family in bed after inspiring and uplifting words or stories, lots of warm hugs, and good night-kisses. Let everyone know that they are loved! Remind them that holy angels are all around!

Mary, My Mother

Dearest Mary, my Mother, thank you for guiding my family each day of our preparation to make our consecration to your Son, Jesus, through your loving hands and Immaculate Heart. Please gather up all of my family's efforts today, as poor as they may be, pouring your graces upon them so that they will be very pleasing to your dear Son. Mother Mary, please protect me as I sleep. We love you. *Hail Mary* . . .

Day 5

Give Praise to God

O humility, lovely flower, I see how few souls
possess you. Is it because you are so beautiful and
at the same time so difficult to attain? O yes, it
is both the one and the other.... The floodgates
of Heaven are open to a humble soul, and a sea
of graces flows upon her.... O Virgin most pure,
but also most humble, help me to attain humility.
Now I understand why there are so few saints;
it is because so few souls are deeply humble.[16]

—Saint Maria Faustina Kowalska

---

[16] *Diary*, no. 1306.

Family Consecration to Jesus through Mary

Morning

Raise your heart and mind to God. Put yourself in His presence. Pray your Morning Offering and the following prayer:

Dear Lord Jesus, I desire to come closer to You. Please help me. Dear Mother Mary, I entrust my entire day to you. Please protect me from the evils of the world. Draw my family close to your Immaculate Heart, help me to be humble, and teach me about your Son. Dear Saint Joseph, help me to learn to be humble. Amen.

Teaching for Parents

Today we continue with Thomas à Kempis.

Only God Is Deserving of Praise

Hence, if I knew well how to cast aside all earthly consolation, either to attain devotion or because of the necessity which, in the absence of human solace, compels me to seek You alone, then I could deservedly hope for Your grace and rejoice in the gift of new consolation.

Thanks be to You from Whom all things come, whenever it is well with me. In Your sight I am vanity and nothingness, a weak, unstable man. In what, therefore, can I glory, and how can I wish to be highly regarded? Is it because I am nothing? This, too, is utterly vain. Indeed, the greatest vanity is the evil plague of empty self-glory, because it draws one away from true glory and robs one of heavenly grace. For when a man is pleased with himself, he displeases You, when he pants after human praise, he is deprived of true virtue. But it is true glory and holy exultation to glory in You and not in self, to rejoice in Your name rather than in one's own virtue, and not to delight in any creature except for Your sake.

Let Your name, not mine, be praised. Let Your work, not mine, be magnified. Let Your holy name be blessed, but let no human praise be given to me. You are my glory. You are the joy of my heart. In You I will glory and rejoice all the day, and for myself I will glory in nothing but my infirmities.[17]

Teaching for Children

Impress upon your children that it is important to recognize who God is and to give glory and praise to Him. We should magnify God's holy name and not ours. Today, again, Thomas à Kempis's words might be very difficult for your youngsters to comprehend. Instead of reading the passage to them, talk to them about the greatness of God and how we should strive to be humble.

Ask your children these questions:

- *Who is God?* God is the Creator of heaven, earth, and all things.
- *Why should we praise and give glory to God?* We should praise and glorify God because He is our Creator and He loves us.
- *Should we want people to praise us?* It's part of our human nature to desire to be liked and praised. We should try not to seek the praise of others, however, so that we can strive to remain humble. God loves the humble and uses them to help in the work of evangelization. Saint Faustina said in today's verse, "The floodgates of Heaven are open to a humble soul."

[17] *Imitation*, bk. 3, chap. 40.

Family Consecration to Jesus through Mary

- *Should we love ourselves more than we love God?* No, we should not love ourselves more than we love God. We should love God most, then others as we love ourselves.
- *Can you think of a reason why it might be dangerous to desire praise for ourselves?* If we desire praise for ourselves, we might get caught up in that desire, thinking mostly of ourselves, and not give God the praise that is due to Him.

Carry Out

Encourage your family to give glory to God during the day by voicing as often as possible, "Glory to You, O Lord!" Another way to give glory to God is to show His great mercy to others in deed, word, or prayer. Ask each family member to carry out at least one work of mercy today, no matter how simple — as long as it is sincere. Help them with this. Ask your family to think about the people who will die today or tonight and to pray that those who are away from God will turn to Him before they die.

Family Prayer

While gathered today, to aid you in your preparation and your emptying yourselves of the spirit of the world, pray the prayers recommended by Saint Louis de Montfort: the Veni Creator Spiritus, the Ave Maris Stella, and the Magnificat. They are found in the appendix "Prayers for Consecration Preparation."

Find time today to pray the holy Rosary.

Evening

Encourage your family to take a few moments to quiet their minds before bed to ponder the day and to ask forgiveness for any mistakes.

Help the little ones with this, pointing out areas in which better efforts are in order for the future. Praise them for their great efforts!

Earnestly strive together to prepare your hearts for your consecration. This is the time to work at emptying yourself of the spirit of the world. Strive for holiness and unplug from unnecessary technology and things of the world. Think about ways to do a better job tomorrow.

End the evening with affirmation and praise, lots of hugs and good-night kisses. Let everyone know that they are loved! As well, before they go to sleep, remind everyone to tell Jesus, Mary, and the saints that they love them too!

Mary, My Mother

Dearest Mary, my Mother, thank you for being with me today as I prepare for my consecration to your Son, Jesus, through your loving hands and your Immaculate Heart. Please teach me humility and look kindly upon and bless my simple efforts today and present them to your dear Son. *Hail Mary* . . .

Day 6

Learn from the Saints

The more a person loves God, the more reason he has to hope in Him. This hope produces in the Saints an unutterable peace, which they preserve even in adversity, because as they love God, and know how beautiful He is to those who love Him, they place all their confidence and find all their repose in Him alone.[18]

—Saint Alphonsus Liguori

---

[18] Quoted in A Parish Priest, *The Teaching Wisdom of the Saints* (N.p.: Aeterna Press, 2015), Kindle ed.

Family Consecration to Jesus through Mary

Morning

Raise your heart and mind to God. Put yourself in His presence. Pray your Morning Offering and the following prayer:

Dear Lord Jesus, I place my trust in You. Help me to pay attention to Your voice today. Dear Mother Mary, help me to strive for sanctity—please grant to me the graces that I need. I offer my day to you, knowing that you will always lead me closer to your Son. Dear Saint Joseph, please help my family as we forge through today. Amen.

Teaching for Parents

Once again, we are instructed by Saint Louis de Montfort to ponder Thomas à Kempis's words in *The Imitation of Christ*, this time with regard to the holy examples of saints.

The Example Set Us by the Holy Fathers

Consider the lively examples set us by the saints, who possessed the light of true perfection and religion, and you will see how little, how nearly nothing, we do. What, alas, is our life, compared with theirs? The saints and friends of Christ served the Lord in hunger and thirst, in cold and nakedness, in work and fatigue, in vigils and fasts, in prayers and holy meditations, in persecutions and many afflictions. How many and severe were the trials they suffered—the Apostles, martyrs, confessors, virgins, and all the rest who willed to follow in the footsteps of Christ! They hated their lives on earth that they might have life in eternity.

How strict and detached were the lives the holy hermits led in the desert! What long and grave temptations they suffered! How often were they beset by the enemy! What frequent and ardent prayers they offered to God! What rigorous fasts they observed! How great their zeal and their love for spiritual perfection! How brave the fight they waged to master their evil habits! What pure and straightforward purpose they showed toward God! By day they labored and by night they spent themselves in long prayers. Even at work they did not cease from mental prayer. They used all their time profitably; every hour seemed too short for serving God, and in the great sweetness of contemplation, they forgot even their bodily needs.

They renounced all riches, dignities, honors, friends, and associates. They desired nothing of the world. They scarcely allowed themselves the necessities of life, and the service of the body, even when necessary, was irksome to them. They were poor in earthly things but rich in grace and virtue.[19]

Teaching for Children

Rather than read the reflection above to your children, teach them in your own words about how the saints strove for sanctity. Let them know that every saint was a "work in progress," just as you are now. They worked hard at holiness, practicing the virtues — even heroic ones. When they fell down, they got up again, confessed their sins, and walked forward in faith.

Impress upon your children the need to try harder to be more pleasing to God. Each day is another opportunity to be good — to practice the virtues, to make loving sacrifices for the love of God

[19] Thomas à Kempis, *Imitation*, bk. 1, chap. 18.

and the conversion of sinners, and to pray more. You can lovingly help your children with this each day.

Begin your teaching by telling your children the story of a saint. Choose one of your favorites, or give them the example of Saint Faustina. Tell them that Saint Faustina was once a simple Polish farm girl, but that God had an important mission for her. She became a nun despite many obstacles. Jesus appeared to the young nun and taught her much about God's great Divine Mercy. Jesus asked Sister Faustina to promote the message of Divine Mercy to the world. She faced many difficulties in carrying out what Jesus had asked of her, but she remained humble and obedient and continued to pray and to trust God, even as she was afflicted with illness, troubling doubts, and feelings of darkness. Because of God's amazing graces and Sister Faustina's cooperation with them, she eventually became a great saint, and the message of Divine Mercy is now known throughout the world.

One time, when the young nun was reading about another saint, she was filled with a great desire that there should be a saint in her own religious congregation. She began to cry, and she asked Jesus why her congregation did not have a saint. Jesus said to her, "Don't cry. You are that saint."[20] We can be deeply inspired by the lives of the saints, who help us to move forward in faith.

Carry Out

Strive to become a saint! Today or sometime soon, help each member of your family to write down a few resolutions. The resolutions can be very simple, such as: "I will persevere when I feel challenged or doubtful"; "I will trust God with all my heart"; "I will spend at

---

[20] Saint Maria Faustina Kowalska, *Diary*, no. 1650.

least fifteen minutes each day away from unnecessary distractions of technology so that I can pray and listen to God."

Ask each family member to place his or her resolution list in a prominent spot (on a bedroom door, in a backpack, on a placemat at the table, and so on).

Family Prayer

While gathered today, to aid you in your preparation and your emptying yourselves of the spirit of the world, pray the prayers recommended by Saint Louis de Montfort: the Veni Creator Spiritus, the Ave Maris Stella, and the Magnificat. They are found in the appendix "Prayers for Consecration Preparation."

Find time today to pray the holy Rosary.

Evening

Help your family ponder the activities and experiences of the day and ask forgiveness for any shortcomings and the blessing of a new day tomorrow to strive for holiness once again. Work hard at emptying yourself of the spirit of the world, as Saint Louis de Montfort has prescribed. Focus your hearts and minds on holiness, and work at spending much less time on the secular.

Offer inspiring and uplifting words or good-night stories, as well as lots of warm hugs and good-night kisses. Let everyone know that they are loved! Let them know too, that holy angels are all around!

Mary, My Mother

Dearest Mary, my Mother, help me to wholeheartedly make my preparation for my consecration to your Son, Jesus, through your loving hands and Immaculate Heart. Please show me how to become a saint. With your help and God's grace, I can. *Hail Mary* . . .

Day 7

Be Obedient

Man's sole duty is to live in obedience
and in the love of his Lord.[21]

—The Blessed Mother to Venerable Mary of Agreda

[21] *Mystical City of God*, vol. 1, no. 725.

Family Consecration to Jesus through Mary

Morning

Raise your heart and mind to God. Put yourself in His presence. Pray your Morning Offering and the following prayer:

Dear Lord Jesus, thank You for Your great love in gifting me with a new day. I want to learn from You. Dear Mother Mary, I entrust my day to you, praying that you will lead my family every step of the way as I prepare to consecrate my life to your Son, Jesus, through your loving hands and Immaculate Heart. Dear Saint Joseph, please show me the way. Amen.

Teaching for Parents

Today, once again we are instructed by Saint Louis de Montfort to ponder Thomas à Kempis's words from *The Imitation of Christ* with regard to the holy examples of saints.

The Example Set Us by the Holy Fathers

Outwardly destitute, inwardly they were full of grace and divine consolation. Strangers to the world, they were close and intimate friends of God. To themselves they seemed as nothing, and they were despised by the world, but in the eyes of God they were precious and beloved. They lived in true humility and simple obedience; they walked in charity and patience, making progress daily on the pathway of spiritual life and obtaining great favor with God.

They were given as an example for all religious, and their power to stimulate us to perfection ought to be greater than that of the lukewarm to tempt us to laxity.

How great was the fervor of all religious in the beginning of their holy institution! How great their devotion in prayer and their rivalry for virtue! What splendid discipline flourished among them! What great reverence and obedience in all things under the rule of a superior! The footsteps they left behind still bear witness that they indeed were holy and perfect men who fought bravely and conquered the world.

Today, he who is not a transgressor and who can bear patiently the duties which he has taken upon himself is considered great. How lukewarm and negligent we are! We lose our original fervor very quickly and we even become weary of life from laziness! Do not you, who have seen so many examples of the devout, fall asleep in the pursuit of virtue![22]

Teaching for Children

Thomas à Kempis mentions the "great reverence and obedience in all things under the rule of a superior." He was describing a religious order. You have a family. Yet you, too, as a parent or a grandparent, require obedience from your children, just as God requires obedience from us, His children.

Impress upon your children the need to listen and obey rules. There are rules from God—the Ten Commandments—there are rules in the Church, and there are rules in your family. Let your children know that the rules are established to keep order, to keep everyone safe, and ultimately to help us to get to Heaven one day.

Choose one of the Ten Commandments and tell the children what it means and how they are to abide by it. It's also a perfect time to go over the rules of the house. Let your children know that the saints followed rules too, and by being obedient, they made

[22] Thomas à Kempis, *Imitation*, bk. 1, chap. 18.

it to Heaven. Their example helps to inspire others to strive for Heaven by choosing to do good.

Finally, today's reading says, "Do not you, who have seen so many examples of the devout, fall asleep in the pursuit of virtue!" Tell your family that each day, and especially now, as they are preparing to make their consecration, that they should "stay awake" and never give up on listening or on following the rules. It will certainly help them to get to Heaven, and their holy example will help others too.

Carry Out

Take a moment today to look at the appendix "Interior and Exterior Practices." See if there is something there that you can soon put into practice as a family. Make it happen!

Family Prayer

While gathered today, to aid you in your preparation and your emptying yourselves of the spirit of the world, pray the prayers recommended by Saint Louis de Montfort: the Veni Creator Spiritus, the Ave Maris Stella, and the Magnificat. They are found in the appendix "Prayers for Consecration Preparation."

Find time today to pray the holy Rosary.

Evening

It's time to ponder the events and encounters of the day and to ask forgiveness for any shortcomings. Thank God for the blessing and promise of a new day tomorrow to move forward once again. Remember that during this special time, you ought to earnestly prepare your heart for your consecration and empty yourself of the spirit of the world. Strive to focus on the teachings and spend less time on the secular during this time of preparation.

Offer inspiring and uplifting words or stories, lots of warm hugs, and good-night kisses. Let everyone know that they are loved! Let them know too, that their guardian angels are with them to protect them!

Mary, My Mother

Dearest Mary, thank you for being my Mother. Please continue to help me prepare my heart to consecrate my life to your Son, Jesus, through your loving hands and Immaculate Heart. Please gather up all of my prayers and efforts today and transfigure them as only you can do, so that they will be worthy to offer to your Son. *Hail Mary* . . .

Day 8

Work Hard at Salvation

Do not human beings
have a hard service on earth,
and are not their days
like the days of a laborer?

—Job 7:1

Morning

Raise your heart and mind to God. Put yourself in His presence.
Pray your Morning Offering and the following prayer:

Dear Lord, Jesus, I come before You as Your little child.
Please guide me to know Your holy will. Dear Mother
Mary, please assist me on my pilgrimage today, helping me
to recognize that I should work very hard at my salvation
and not waste the opportunities set before me, in which
I am to serve lovingly and grow in holiness. Dear Saint
Joseph, I have no doubt that you will help and guide my
family. Amen.

Teaching for Parents

We are instructed by Saint Louis de Montfort to ponder Thomas
à Kempis's words from *The Imitation of Christ* with regard to resisting temptation.

Resisting Temptation

So long as we live in this world we cannot escape suffering
and temptation. Whence it is written in Job: "The life of
man upon earth is a warfare." Everyone, therefore, must
guard against temptation and must watch in prayer lest the
devil, who never sleeps but goes about seeking whom he may
devour, find occasion to deceive him. No one is so perfect
or so holy but he is sometimes tempted; man cannot be
altogether free from temptation.

Yet temptations, though troublesome and severe, are
often useful to a man, for in them he is humbled, purified,

and instructed. The saints all passed through many temptations and trials to profit by them, while those who could not resist became reprobate and fell away. There is no state so holy, no place so secret that temptations and trials will not come. Man is never safe from them as long as he lives, for they come from within us — in sin we were born. When one temptation or trial passes, another comes; we shall always have something to suffer because we have lost the state of original blessedness.

Many people try to escape temptations, only to fall more deeply. We cannot conquer simply by fleeing, but by patience and true humility we become stronger than all our enemies. The man who only shuns temptations outwardly and does not uproot them will make little progress; indeed they will quickly return, more violent than before.

Little by little, in patience and long-suffering you will overcome them, by the help of God rather than by severity and your own rash ways. Often take counsel when tempted; and do not be harsh with others who are tempted, but console them as you yourself would wish to be consoled.

The beginning of all temptation lies in a wavering mind and little trust in God, for as a rudderless ship is driven hither and yon by waves, so a careless and irresolute man is tempted in many ways.[23]

Teaching for Children

There is so much wisdom in today's teaching from Thomas à Kempis! First of all, we should know that we can never escape the temptations in this world. We will certainly be able to resist them,

[23] Thomas à Kempis, *Imitation*, bk. 1, chap. 13.

however, with God's grace. As well, we should know that life is really a battle against evil and to gain everlasting life in Heaven. For the most part, the battle is invisible, so we might not always pay attention. But we must!

Talk to your children today about the need to work hard at our salvation. That means that each day and throughout the day, we are presented with a variety of choices. What will we choose? The way that pleases God and brings us closer to Heaven? Or, will we fall into temptation to do something that is wrong? Give your children some examples.

Tell your children that we cannot escape temptations in life (because they are always present) but that we do have the power in our will to choose to do what is good. This might be a good time to talk to your children about peer pressure and why it is important always to choose the "high road" and not allow ourselves to become influenced by people and things that go against our beliefs. It is important to surround ourselves with like-minded, faith-filled friends whenever possible. They will help us on our journey through life.

Let your children know that we will face temptations every day in some way, but we should be encouraged to know that God wants us to be happy with Him in Heaven for all eternity. He will always help us to choose to do what is right and good. But we must be close to God and talk to Him often in prayer. We need to ask for His help, for we most certainly need it.

Carry Out

Ask Saint Michael to protect your family. Your children might not fully understand, but it's essential to teach them about the spiritual realm. There are indeed good and holy angels who protect us, including our guardian angels! We need to call upon them very often.

Here are two additional prayers for today:

Saint Michael the Archangel, defend us in battle. Be our defense against the wickedness and snares of the Devil. May God rebuke him, we humbly pray, and do thou, O Prince of the heavenly hosts, by the power of God, thrust into hell Satan and all the evil spirits who prowl about the world seeking the ruin of souls. Amen.

O glorious prince Saint Michael, chief and commander of the heavenly hosts, guardian of souls, vanquisher of rebel spirits, servant in the house of the Divine King, and our admirable conductor, you who shine with excellence and superhuman virtue, deliver us, who turn to you with confidence, from all evil and enable us by your gracious protection to serve God more and more faithfully every day. Amen.

Family Prayer

While gathered today, to aid you in your preparation and your emptying yourselves of the spirit of the world, pray the prayers recommended by Saint Louis de Montfort: the Veni Creator Spiritus, the Ave Maris Stella, and the Magnificat. They are found in the appendix "Prayers for Consecration Preparation."

Find time today to pray the holy Rosary.

Evening

Day is done. It's time to ponder the day and ask forgiveness for any shortcomings and the blessing of a new day tomorrow to strive for holiness once again. Encourage the children to talk to you about their day. During this distinctive time of consecration preparation, you can keep in mind the need to empty yourself of the spirit of the world. Ask Mother Mary for the graces.

As always, put everyone to bed on a positive note. Bless them with Holy Water. Offer inspiring and uplifting words or stories, affirmation, lots of warm hugs, and good night kisses. Let everyone know that they are loved! Let them know too, that holy Angels are all around!

Mary, My Mother

Dearest Mary, my Mother, thank you for guiding me this day as I prepare to make my consecration to your Son, Jesus, through your loving hands and Immaculate Heart. Please help me to be strong in resisting temptations and much more attentive to the spiritual life. *Hail Mary* . . .

Day 9

Resist Temptation

When tempted, invoke your Angel. He is more
eager to help you than you are to be helped! Ignore
the devil and do not be afraid of him: He trembles
and flees at your Guardian Angel's sight.[24]

—Saint John Bosco

---

[24] Quoted in Joan Carroll Cruz, *Angels and Devils* (Charlotte, NC:
TAN Books, 1999), Kindle ed.

Family Consecration to Jesus through Mary

Morning

Raise your heart and mind to God. Put yourself in His presence. Pray your Morning Offering and the following prayer:

Dear Lord Jesus, I give praise to You for the morning—a new gift, an empty slate, an opportunity for much grace. Please guide me this day and make straight my crooked lines. Dear Mother Mary, please grant to me the graces that I need most to resist temptations today. I entrust my entire day to you. Dear Saint Joseph, lead me and protect me. Amen.

Teaching for Parents

Today we continue to read Thomas à Kempis's words on resisting temptation.

Resisting Temptation

Fire tempers iron and temptation steels the just. Often we do not know what we can stand, but temptation shows us what we are.

Above all, we must be especially alert against the beginnings of temptation, for the enemy is more easily conquered if he is refused admittance to the mind and is met beyond the threshold when he knocks.

Someone has said very aptly: "Resist the beginnings; remedies come too late, when by long delay the evil has gained strength." First, a mere thought comes to mind, then strong imagination, followed by pleasure, evil delight, and consent. Thus, because he is not resisted in the beginning,

Satan gains full entry. And the longer a man delays in resisting, so much the weaker does he become each day, while the strength of the enemy grows against him.

Some suffer great temptations in the beginning of their conversion, others toward the end, while some are troubled almost constantly throughout their life. Others, again, are tempted but lightly according to the wisdom and justice of Divine Providence, Who weighs the status and merit of each and prepares all for the salvation of His elect.

We should not despair, therefore, when we are tempted, but pray to God the more fervently that He may see fit to help us, for according to the word of Paul, He will make issue with temptation that we may be able to bear it. Let us humble our souls under the hand of God in every trial and temptation, for He will save and exalt the humble in spirit.

In temptations and trials the progress of a man is measured; in them opportunity for merit and virtue is made more manifest.[25]

Teaching for Children

We learn about resisting and conquering temptation today. Specifically, we should pay attention to these words: "Above all, we must be especially alert against the beginnings of temptation, for the enemy is more easily conquered if he is refused admittance to the mind and is met beyond the threshold when he knocks." Wise words indeed! In order to be able to resist at the beginning, we must have firm knowledge of what is right and what is wrong.

---

[25] Thomas à Kempis, *Imitation*, bk. 1, chap. 13.

That is why parents and grandparents, as the first and foremost educators in the Faith, must step up to the plate to teach their children.

Begin today's teaching by giving your children three examples of situations in which they must choose right from wrong. One might be of a small child in a candy store. He really wants that candy cane that he sees. Should he take it when no one is looking? Ask the children why he shouldn't do so.

After giving a couple of other examples, ask your children to share a situation in which they had to make a choice between right or wrong. Discuss it as a family.

Once again, impress upon them that life is filled with opportunities to choose and that it is everyone's responsibility to learn the Faith and practice it fully, no matter what others are doing. On top of that, we not only try to make it to Heaven ourselves; we pray for others and always set a good example. You might feel inclined to go a bit further and describe for your children an instance in which their example in choosing to do the right thing could help another person to choose to resist temptation too.

Finally, tell your children that the best way to fight the temptation to do something contrary to their Faith (sin) is to fight the temptation right from the start so that we do not allow the evil one to get a foothold. Always pray for the grace you need.

Carry Out

As a work of mercy, ask your family members to think about something they can do for a person who has wronged them. Even though that person chose to do something that was not right, we can choose to do something good. It might be to let the person know that we forgive him or her. It might be to pray for that person. Talk about it and help the children to come up with a safe and holy plan.

Family Prayer

While gathered today, to aid you in your preparation and your emptying yourselves of the spirit of the world, pray the prayers recommended by Saint Louis de Montfort: the Veni Creator Spiritus, the Ave Maris Stella, and the Magnificat. They are found in the appendix "Prayers for Consecration Preparation."

Find time today to pray the holy Rosary.

Evening

The sun has set, and it's time to ponder your day. Help and encourage your family members to quiet their minds before bed to pause and ponder the day and ask forgiveness for any shortcomings. Help your children to see any areas in which better efforts are in order for the future. Always praise them for their great efforts!

Earnestly strive to prepare your hearts for your consecration. This is the time to work at emptying yourself of the spirit of the world. Strive for holiness and unplug from unnecessary technology and the things of the world during this time of preparation.

End the evening with a blessing with holy water before going to bed. Read or tell an inspiring saint story, and give lots of hugs and good-night kisses. Let everyone know that they are loved! Remind them that holy angels are all around and their guardian angels are watching over them.

Mary, My Mother

Dearest Mary, our Mother, I am getting ready to conse-crate my life to your Son through you. Please continue to guide me each day. Be with me as I sleep. I love you! *Hail Mary* . . .

Day 10

Serve God, Not the World

God did not tell us to follow Him because
He needed our help, but because He knew
that loving Him would make us whole.[26]

—St. Irenaeus of Lyons

---

[26] Quoted in *My Daily Catholic Bible: New Testament, NABRE:
10-Minute Daily Readings*, ed. Paul Thigpen (Huntington, IN: Our
Sunday Visitor, 2008), Kindle ed.

Family Consecration to Jesus through Mary

Morning

Raise your heart and mind to God. Put yourself in His presence. Pray your Morning Offering and the following prayer:

Dear Lord Jesus, here I am, trusting in You and desiring to serve. Please open my heart to Your love and mercy. I want to be Your true disciple. Dear Mother Mary and Saint Joseph, please stay with me and show me the way to Jesus. Amen.

Teaching for Parents

Today we read Thomas à Kempis's words on serving God and despising the world.

To Despise the World and Serve God Is Sweet

Now again I will speak, Lord, and will not be silent. I will speak to the hearing of my God, my Lord, and my King Who is in heaven. How great, O Lord, is the multitude of Your mercies which You have stored up for those who love You. But what are You to those who love You? What are You to those who serve You with their whole heart?

Truly beyond the power of words is the sweetness of contemplation You give to those who love You. To me You have shown the sweetness of Your charity, especially in having made me when I did not exist, in having brought me back to serve You when I had gone far astray from You, in having commanded me to love You.

O Fountain of unceasing love, what shall I say of You? How can I forget You, Who have been pleased to remember me even after I had wasted away and perished? You have shown mercy to Your servant beyond all hope, and have exhibited grace and friendship beyond his deserving.

What return shall I make to You for this grace? For it is not given every man to forsake all things, to renounce the world, and undertake the religious life. Is it anything great that I should serve You, Whom every creature is bound to serve? It should not seem much to me; instead it should appear great and wonderful that You condescend to receive into Your service one who is so poor and unworthy. Behold, all things are Yours, even those which I have and by which I serve You. Behold, heaven and earth, which You created for the service of man, stand ready, and each day they do whatever You command. But even this is little, for You have appointed angels also to minister to man — yea, more than all this — You Yourself have condescended to serve man and have promised to give him Yourself.

What return shall I make for all these thousands of benefits? Would that I could serve You all the days of my life! Would that for but one day I could serve You worthily! Truly You are worthy of all service, all honor, and everlasting praise. Truly You are my Lord, and I am Your poor servant, bound to serve You with all my powers, praising You without ever becoming weary. I wish to do this — this is my desire.... Supply whatever is wanting in me.

It is a great honor, a great glory to serve You and to despise all things for Your sake. They who give themselves gladly to Your most holy service will possess great grace. They who cast aside all carnal delights for Your love will find the most sweet consolation of the Holy Ghost.[27]

---

[27] Thomas à Kempis, *Imitation*, bk. 3, chap. 10.

Family Consecration to Jesus through Mary

Teaching for Children

Talk to your children about striving to be Our Lord's disciple. What does that mean? Being Jesus' disciple means believing in and loving Him. We want to follow Him and tell others about Him.

Tell your children that to be Jesus' disciple is the best thing in the world, but it is also difficult at times. That is mostly because many people do not believe in Jesus and do not want to live holy lives. They have succumbed to the temptations of the world and have chosen to live sinful lives. Remind your children that you recently talked about temptations and how to resist them with God's help. Tell them that because many people choose to live unholy lifestyles, they can become hostile toward Christians. Even so, we should pray for them because God wants us to. Our prayers and works of mercy can help convert their hearts.

Finally, what is the great gift that Jesus gave to all of His disciples until the end of time when He was hanging on the Cross? His own Mother! He said, "Here is your Mother" (John 19:27) to His disciple John, who represented all of His disciples until the end of the world. Mother Mary helps us with the graces that she bestows upon us. She helps us to be her Son's disciples. She will without doubt help you to make your consecration.

Carry Out

Encourage your family to pray three extra Hail Marys today for those in our world who have chosen not to follow Jesus and for those who do not yet know Him. As well, ask your children to try their best to be wonderful Christian examples to others, even when it is difficult to do so.

Family Prayer

While gathered today, to aid you in your preparation and your emptying yourselves of the spirit of the world, pray the prayers recommended by Saint Louis de Montfort: the Veni Creator Spiritus, the Ave Maris Stella, and the Magnificat. They are found in the appendix "Prayers for Consecration Preparation."

Find time today to pray the holy Rosary.

Evening

Another day of earnestly striving to together prepare your hearts for your family Marian consecration is coming to an end. You have worked at emptying yourself of the spirit of the world. Encourage your family members to pause a moment before bed to ponder the day and ask forgiveness for any shortcomings. Help your children and always praise them for their great efforts!

End the evening with a blessing with holy water before going to bed. Consider reading an inspiring saint story or tell a story. Give plenty of warm hugs and good-night kisses. Let everyone know that they are loved! Remind them that holy angels are all around and their guardian angels are watching over them. Remember, "They who give themselves gladly" to Jesus' "most holy service will possess great grace."

Mary, My Mother

Dearest Mary, thank you for being my Mother. Thank you for helping me with my preparation to make my consecration to your Son, Jesus, through your loving hands and Immaculate Heart. Please show me how to be true disciples of your Son. *Hail Mary . . .*

Day 11

Amend Your Life

Our progress in holiness depends on God and
ourselves — on God's grace and on our will to be
holy. We must have a real living determination
to reach holiness. "I will be a saint" means I will
despoil myself of all that is not God; I will strip my
heart of all created things; I will live in poverty
and detachment; I will renounce my will, my
inclinations, my whims and fancies, and make
myself a willing slave to the will of God.[28]

—Mother Teresa

[28] Mother Teresa, A Gift for God: Prayers and Meditations, compiled
by Malcolm Muggeridge, repr. ed. (New York: HarperOne, 2003),
84.

Family Consecration to Jesus through Mary

Morning

Raise your heart and mind to God. Put yourself in His presence. Pray your Morning Offering and the following prayer:

Dear Lord Jesus, I place my trust in Your loving mercy. Please guide me this day. Dear Mother Mary, take me as your little child and teach me the ways of holiness. I want to become a saint! I entrust my day to you. Dear Saint Joseph, please protect and lead my family. Amen.

Teaching for Parents

Today we learn about the need to strive for perfection in the spiritual life and are reminded of the essential work involved.

Zeal in Amending our Lives

Be watchful and diligent in God's service and often think of why you left the world and came here. Was it not that you might live for God and become a spiritual man? Strive earnestly for perfection, then, because in a short time you will receive the reward of your labor, and neither fear nor sorrow shall come upon you at the hour of death.

Labor a little now, and soon you shall find great rest, in truth, eternal joy; for if you continue faithful and diligent in doing, God will undoubtedly be faithful and generous in rewarding. Continue to have reasonable hope of gaining salvation, but do not act as though you were certain of it, lest you grow indolent and proud.

One day when a certain man who wavered often and anxiously between hope and fear was struck with sadness, he knelt in humble prayer before the altar of a church. While meditating on these things, he said: "Oh if I but knew whether I should persevere to the end!" Instantly he heard within the divine answer: "If you knew this, what would you do? Do now what you would do then and you will be quite secure." Immediately consoled and comforted, he resigned himself to the divine will and the anxious uncertainty ceased. His curiosity no longer sought to know what the future held for him, and he tried instead to find the perfect, the acceptable will of God in the beginning and end of every good work.

"Trust thou in the Lord and do good," says the Prophet, "dwell in the land and thou shalt feed on its riches."

There is one thing that keeps many from zealously improving their lives, that is, dread of the difficulty, the toil of battle. Certainly they who try bravely to overcome the most difficult and unpleasant obstacles far outstrip others in the pursuit of virtue. A man makes the most progress and merits the most grace precisely in those matters wherein he gains the greatest victories over self and most mortifies his will. True, each one has his own difficulties to meet and conquer, but a diligent and sincere man will make greater progress even though he have more passions than one who is more even-tempered but less concerned about virtue.[29]

Teaching for Children

Thomas à Kempis speaks of laboring now on earth so as one day to enjoy eternal rest in Heaven. In the verse that begins our reflection today, Mother Teresa reminds us, "We must have a real living

[29] Thomas à Kempis, *Imitation*, bk. 1, chap. 25.

determination to reach holiness." Then she enumerates the ways in which we do this. Progressing in the spiritual life is not for the faint of heart! But, is there any other way to Heaven? No, there is not. We must work hard at our salvation. We can't sit still and expect every grace and virtue to fall into our laps with no efforts on our part. This doesn't mean that because it is arduous, we won't experience joy in this life on earth. We surely will possess joy even throughout the difficult moments.

Talk to your children about the importance of being serious about our spiritual lives. Although you will, of course, take into consideration their ages and their level of understanding, everyone can learn that it is important to pray and nourish our faith daily in order to reach Heaven one day. Tell your children that God is very pleased with our efforts to grow closer to Him and to pray for and care about others. He wants us to love Him above all and love others as ourselves. Jesus taught His disciples, "You shall love the Lord your God with all your heart, and with all your soul, and with all your mind.' This is the greatest and first commandment. And a second is like it: 'You shall love your neighbor as yourself'" (Matt. 22:37–39).

Let the children know that if we love God and neighbor as we should, we should work hard to achieve a holy life. Ask some questions such as these:

- Can you snap your fingers and make a beautiful three-layer cake, ready to enjoy, appear instantly on the kitchen table?
- Can you cause a snowman suddenly to be built outside on a winter's day by waving a wand?
- Does your homework paper write itself?
- Do you know the story before you read the book?

The answers to all of these questions is the same: no. We must put in the effort to create something or to make something happen. Tell your children that it's the same in our spiritual lives. We need to work hard each day at praying, doing good, offering God's mercy to others, and so on.

I am reminded of St. John Paul II, who said, "If an ear is to grow or a flower blossom, there are times which cannot be forced; for the birth of a human being, nine months are required; to write a book or a worthy piece of music, years must often be spent in patient searching. This is also the law of the spirit.... To encounter the mystery takes patience, inner purification, silence and waiting."[30]

Carry Out

Encourage your family to work harder today to be good to one another even when it is difficult. Ask them to pray a sincere prayer today asking the Blessed Mother for the graces to overcome obstacles bravely and to possess a greater desire for holiness.

Family Prayer

While gathered today, to aid you in your preparation and your emptying yourselves of the spirit of the world, pray the prayers recommended by Saint Louis de Montfort: the Veni Creator Spiritus, the Ave Maris Stella, and the Magnificat. They are found in the appendix "Prayers for Consecration Preparation."

Find time today to pray the holy Rosary.

Evening

Evening has arrived. Help and encourage your family members to ponder the day and ask forgiveness for any shortcomings. Help

---

[30] St. John Paul II, General Audience, July 26, 2000.

your children to see any areas in which better efforts are in order for the future. Always praise them for their great efforts!

Continue to strive for holiness and unplug from unnecessary technology during this distinctive time of preparation as you work at emptying yourself of the spirit of the world.

Bless the family with holy water before going to bed. Send everyone to bed with hugs and kisses, emphasizing that they are loved! Remind them to pray to their guardian angels.

Mary, My Mother

Dearest Mary, my Mother, thank you for being with me this day and for all of your help in my consecration preparation. Please gather up all of my efforts and prayers today and turn them into a beautiful bouquet for your dear Son. *Hail Mary* . . .

Day 12

Be Fervent

Let us ask our Lady to make our hearts "meek and
humble" as her Son's was. It is so very easy to be
proud and harsh and selfish—so easy; but we have
been created for greater things. How much we can
learn from our Lady! She was so humble because she
was all for God. She was full of grace. Tell our Lady to
tell Jesus: "They have no wine; they need the wine of
humility and meekness, of kindness and sweetness."
She is sure to tell us, "Do whatever He tells you."[31]

—Mother Teresa

---

[31] *A Gift for God*, 57.

Family Consecration to Jesus through Mary

Morning

Raise your heart and mind to God. Put yourself in His presence. Pray your Morning Offering and the following prayer:

Dear Lord, Jesus, I praise You for the gift of my life and this new day in which to serve You and others. Dear Mother Mary, please protect me and my family from the dangers of the darkened culture. Help us to keep our eyes on Heaven and its rewards. Dear Saint Joseph, please help my family as we prepare to make our consecration to Jesus through Mary. Amen.

Teaching for Parents

Today is the last day of the "emptying out of the spirit of the world" phase of your consecration preparation. Saint Louis de Montfort prescribes the following reading on amending our lives:

Making the Most of Opportunities

Make the best of every opportunity, so that if you see or hear good example you may be moved to imitate it. On the other hand, take care lest you be guilty of those things which you consider reprehensible, or if you have ever been guilty of them, try to correct yourself as soon as possible.

As you see others, so they see you. How pleasant and sweet to behold brethren fervent and devout, well mannered and disciplined! How sad and painful to see them wandering in dissolution, not practicing the things to which they are called! How hurtful it is to neglect the purpose of their vocation and to attend to what is not their business!

Remember the purpose you have undertaken, and keep in mind the image of the Crucified. Even though you may have walked for many years on the pathway to God, you may well be ashamed if, with the image of Christ before you, you do not try to make yourself still more like Him.

The religious who concerns himself intently and devoutly with our Lord's most holy life and Passion will find there an abundance of all things useful and necessary for him. He need not seek for anything better than Jesus. If the Crucified should come to our hearts, how quickly and abundantly we would learn! ...

A fervent and diligent man is ready for all things. It is greater work to resist vices and passions than to sweat in physical toil. He who does not overcome small faults shall fall little by little into greater ones.

If you have spent the day profitably, you will always be happy at eventide. Watch over yourself, arouse yourself, warn yourself, and regardless of what becomes of others, do not neglect yourself. The more violence you do to yourself, the more progress you will make.[32]

Teaching for Children

We learn today about the need to amend our lives, to be careful not to fall under bad influences, and to strive to follow good examples. Thomas à Kempis tells us, "Make the best of every opportunity, so that if you see or hear good example you may be moved to imitate it. On the other hand, take care lest you be guilty of those things which you consider reprehensible, or if you have ever been guilty of them, try to correct yourself as soon as possible."

[32] Thomas à Kempis, *Imitation*, bk. 1, chap. 25.

Family Consecration to Jesus through Mary

Tell your children that they are always surrounded with ex-amples — good ones and bad ones. Give them some instances. You might mention games, books, or television shows that they aren't allowed to have or to watch because they are not wholesome or because they are contrary to your beliefs. Explain to them that if we surround ourselves with people who don't care about the Faith or about being good, and if we use things or watch content that is against our beliefs, eventually, these things might cause us to stumble and fall. In other words, we need to pay attention to our surroundings and partake only in safe and wholesome things approved by parents and grandparents. It's important not to get involved with our friends' items that might lead us astray from the road to Heaven. Use simple yet descriptive examples to drive home your teachings.

Let your children know that their hard work in the spiritual life will surely pay off, and as Thomas à Kempis said, if we have "spent the day profitably, [we] will always be happy at eventide."

Here's to a very good day of trying hard and a happy evening!

Carry Out

Today, or sometime soon, have your children make some colorful greeting cards out of paper and crayons or markers. Help them to write hopeful loving messages about God. Devise a way to send them out or deliver them to those who could use a lift.

Family Prayer

On this last day of our "emptying out of the spirit of the world," we continue with Saint Louis de Montfort's recommendation to pray the following prayers: the Veni Creator Spiritus, the Ave

Maris Stella, and the Magnificat. They are found in the appendix "Prayers for Consecration Preparation."

Find time today to pray the holy Rosary.

Evening

Evening is here. It's time to ponder the events and encounters of the day and to ask forgiveness for any shortcomings. Help the children with this. Thank God for the hope and blessing of a new day tomorrow to move forward once again in earnestly preparing your hearts for your family Marian consecration. Strive to focus on the teachings and spend less time on unnecessary technology and distractions during this distinctive time of preparation.

Bless your family with holy water, and offer inspiring and uplifting words or stories, lots of warm hugs, and good-night kisses. Let everyone know that they are loved!

Mary, My Mother

Dearest Mary, my Mother, thank you for being with me as I move closer to my consecration to your Son, Jesus, through your loving hands and Immaculate Heart. Please take me by the hand and lead me to your Son. *Hail Mary* . . .

Family Activity for Part 1

Your family has completed the twelve-day period of emptying themselves of "the spirit of the world." Though, tomorrow, you will go straight into the next phase, which is "Obtaining Knowledge of Self," take time soon to pause and, in a sense, celebrate together. One way is to totally unplug from unnecessary technology and enjoy playing a board game together; or, if not a board game, then perhaps, weather permitting, a family walk or hike. Still another idea is to all curl up together to read a good storybook. Or how about a dish of ice cream?

These are fun, wholesome activities to be enjoyed anytime. I'm sure I don't have to tell you, however, that life is busy and that it's often tough to carve out time to be still and enjoy one another's company. That is why I suggest that you plan to pause and celebrate, even very simply, that you have finished the first phase.

Part 2

Obtaining Knowledge of Yourself

Saint Louis de Montfort instructs us that in order to achieve union
with Jesus, we must examine our lives, renounce our wills, have
contrition for our sins, and do it all at the feet of Mary. Our Mother
will give us the light to know ourselves better. Being near the
Blessed Mother in prayer through your preparation will help im-
mensely. Though we will see ourselves as unworthy and sinful,
Mary's motherly love will sustain us and lead us closer to her Son,
Jesus. This is a time to reflect and to pray deeply with Mary's help.

This period's spiritual exercises: pray, examine your conscience,
reflect, make acts of renunciation of your will and acts of contrition for your sins—all with Mary's help. She will help you to
know yourself truly.

Day 13

Persevere in Prayer

So I say to you, Ask, and it will be given you;
search, and you will find; knock, and the door
will be opened for you. For everyone who asks
receives, and everyone who searches finds, and for
everyone who knocks, the door will be opened.

—Luke 11:9–10

Morning

Raise your heart and mind to God. Put yourself in His presence. Pray your Morning Offering and the following prayer:

Dear Lord Jesus, thank You for caring for me through the night and gifting me with a brand-new day. Please protect me from the evil that threatens to get in the way of my walk today. Dear Mother Mary, help me to be attentive to serving lovingly those God calls me to serve: my family and my neighbor. Lead me through this day of preparation. I entrust our day to your care. Saint Joseph, I need your holy help. Amen.

Teaching for Parents

From today's readings, we learn to pray effectively and to persevere in prayer.

The Lord's Prayer

He was praying in a certain place, and after he had finished, one of his disciples said to him, "Lord, teach us to pray, as John taught his disciples." He said to them, "When you pray, say:

Father, hallowed be your name.

Your kingdom come.

Give us each day our daily bread.

And forgive us our sins,

for we ourselves forgive everyone indebted to us.

And do not bring us to the time of trial." (Luke 11:1–4)

Perseverance in Prayer

And he said to them, "Suppose one of you has a friend, and you go to him at midnight and say to him, 'Friend, lend me three loaves of bread; or a friend of mine has arrived, and I have nothing to set before him.' And he answers from within, 'Do not bother me; the door has already been locked, and my children are with me in bed; I cannot get up and give you anything.' I tell you, even though he will not get up and give him anything because he is his friend, at least because of his persistence he will get up and give him whatever he needs." (Luke 11:5–8)

Effective Prayer

So I say to you, Ask, and it will be given you; search, and you will find; knock, and the door will be opened for you. For everyone who asks receives, and everyone who searches finds, and for everyone who knocks, the door will be opened. (Luke 11:9–10)

Teaching for Children

Today's teaching deals with kinds of prayer. First, Jesus teaches His disciples the Lord's Prayer. He does this in response to a request from one of the disciples. Second, we have a Scripture passage that teaches us about persevering in prayer. In this parable, Jesus teaches that we shouldn't give up on prayer; rather, we should persevere. Third, we are taught about asking, knocking, and searching. Jesus assures us that "everyone who asks receives, and everyone who searches finds, and for everyone who knocks, the door will be opened."

Pray the Lord's Prayer slowly with your children.

Our Father, who art in Heaven, hallowed be Thy Name. Thy Kingdom come. Thy will be done on earth, as it is in Heaven. Give us this day our daily bread, and forgive us our trespasses, as we forgive those who trespass against us, and lead us not into temptation, but deliver us from evil.

Then go through it line by line and explain its meaning. Let your children know that God wants us to pray to Him, to thank Him, to ask Him for help and for our needs and the needs of others. Tell them that God insists that we forgive those who have wronged us or wronged others. We are not saying that the wrongs that others have done are acceptable. But we must forgive the offenses, and we should pray for the souls of those who committed them.

Read to your children the second reading above, "Perseverance in Prayer." It should be simple enough for their understanding. If not, explain that it is important to persevere in anything worthwhile, especially prayer. You can use the analogy of the "squeaky wheel that gets the grease."

Finally, reassure your children with the last verse above about "Effective Prayer." Let them know that we should ask God for the things that are good for our bodies and souls. Not every prayer is answered in the manner that we might wish. Sometimes, God's answer is "Not now." Sometimes it might be "No, not at all." Why is this? Because God knows exactly what is best for our lives. We have to trust Him.

Carry Out

Ask your family to pray their prayers a bit slower and not to rush through them. Tell them that prayer is their special time with God. He is our true Friend (with a capital F)! We want to show Him that we love Him, as well as our dear Mother Mary, Saint

Joseph, and all the angels and the saints. Slow down and pray more wholeheartedly.

Family Prayer

Saint Louis prescribes three prayers for today and throughout this phase of preparation. They are the Litany of the Holy Spirit, the Litany of the Blessed Virgin, and the Ave Maris Stella. You will find them in the appendix "Prayers for Consecration Preparation."

Find time today to pray the holy Rosary.

Evening

As evening falls, it's time to ponder the events and encounters of the day and to ask forgiveness for any shortcomings. Thank God for the promise and blessing of a new day tomorrow to try once again. Remember that during this special time, you ought to prepare your heart earnestly for your consecration and pray that you will recognize and discover knowledge of yourself during this week of preparation. Strive to focus on the teachings provided and spend less time on anything that will distract you from this preparation.

End the evening on a positive note, and offer inspiring and uplifting words or stories, lots of warm hugs, and good-night kisses. Let everyone know that they are loved! Let them know too, that their guardian angels are with them to protect them!

Family Consecration to Jesus through Mary

Mary, My Mother

Dearest Mary, my Mother, thank you for being with my family as we prepare to make our family Marian consecration to your Son, Jesus, through your loving hands and Immaculate Heart. Teach me to be humble as I move through this week. Be with me tonight with your holy protective mantle wrapped around us as I sleep. I love you. *Hail Mary* . . .

Day 14

Cast Away Pride

A little drop of simple obedience is worth
a million times more than a whole vase
full of the choicest contemplation.[33]

—Saint Mary Magdalen de' Pazzi

---

[33] Quoted in Anthony Vincent Bruno, *The Wisdom of the Saints* (self-pub., 2019), Kindle ed.

Morning

Raise your heart and mind to God. Put yourself in His presence.
Pray your Morning Offering and the following prayer:

Dear Lord Jesus, thank You for Your amazing love, which
I cannot fully comprehend right now. I desire to love
You more and bring others to You. Dear Mother Mary,
open my heart and help me to be attentive to serving
lovingly those in need. I offer my heart to you. Please
mold it to be more like yours — humble, loving, and
obedient. Saint Joseph, head of the Holy Family, please
help me. Amen.

Teaching for Parents

Today's reading from Thomas à Kempis stresses the importance of
working hard to humble ourselves and rid ourselves of pride.

------

*The Obedience of One Humbly Subject
to the Example of Jesus Christ*

The voice of Christ:
My child, he who attempts to escape obeying withdraws
himself from grace. Likewise he who seeks private benefits
for himself loses those which are common to all. He who
does not submit himself freely and willingly to his superior,
shows that his flesh is not yet perfectly obedient but that it
often rebels and murmurs against him.

Learn quickly, then, to submit yourself to your superior
if you wish to conquer your own flesh. For the exterior
enemy is more quickly overcome if the inner man is not

laid waste. There is no more troublesome, no worse enemy of the soul than you yourself, if you are not in harmony with the spirit. It is absolutely necessary that you conceive a true contempt for yourself if you wish to be victorious over flesh and blood.

Because you still love yourself too inordinately, you are afraid to resign yourself wholly to the will of others. Is it such a great matter if you, who are but dust and nothingness, subject yourself to man for the sake of God, when I, the All-Powerful, the Most High, Who created all things out of nothing, humbly subjected Myself to man for your sake? I became the most humble and the lowest of all men that you might overcome your pride with My humility.

Learn to obey, you who are but dust! Learn to humble yourself, you who are but earth and clay, and bow down under the foot of every man! Learn to break your own will, to submit to all subjection!

Be zealous against yourself! Allow no pride to dwell in you, but prove yourself so humble and lowly that all may walk over you and trample upon you as dust in the streets!

What have you, vain man, to complain of? What answer can you make, vile sinner, to those who accuse you, you who have so often offended God and so many times deserved hell? But My eye has spared you because your soul was precious in My sight, so that you might know My love and always be thankful for My benefits, so that you might give yourself continually to true subjection and humility, and might patiently endure contempt.[34]

---

[34] Thomas à Kempis, *Imitation*, bk. 3, chap. 13.

Teaching for Children

In today's reading, Thomas à Kempis writes in the "voice of Christ." He talks about our own selves as the enemies of our souls. His words are strong. They need to be. Our world these days is very far from God. Today's message suggests that we humble ourselves and rid ourselves of pride. If we have superiors in our lives (in addition to God), we need to listen to and obey them. The saints have consistently shown us that obedience is key in the spiritual life. Yet it's a tough virtue to acquire. Saint Francis de Sales explains why: "We all have a natural inclination to command, and a great aversion to obey; and yet, it is certain that it is more to our advantage to obey than to command. It is for this reason that perfect souls have so great an affection for obedience, and find in it all their delight."[35]

In today's verse we read what Saint Mary Magdalen de' Pazzi thinks about obedience. She had a determined regard for the virtue of obedience. She knew it could guard her from the danger of doing her own will, rather than God's will. When she operated under obedience to her superiors, she was wholeheartedly confident that by doing so, her peace and serenity would be restored whenever she endured strenuous trials.

It is said that, one day, Saint Frances of Rome was reciting the Office of the Blessed Virgin and was interrupted by her husband, who called for her four times while she was praying the same antiphon. Each time, Saint Frances answered her husband promptly. When she returned to her prayer book after the fourth time, she found that the antiphon was written in gold letters! Can we imagine this?

[35] Quoted in *A Year with the Saints: Catholic Virtues* (Charlotte, NC: TAN Books, n.d.), June 1, http://www.catholictradition.org/Saints/virtue6.htm.

With these holy teachings and stories under your belt, talk to your children today about the need for obedience. Start with the Fourth Commandment, which tells us to honor our fathers and mothers. Expand upon your teaching, letting your children know that God knows what is best for us and gives us superiors who will teach and guide us. Above all, God is our greatest superior. We must obey His commandments. We must obey our parents' rules too, for our parents stand in place of God.

Carry Out

Read the verse that begins today's reflections. Obedience requires humility. When gathered at the dinner table tonight, ask your family members to give a few examples of how our culture today disobeys the laws of our Lord. Help them by giving the first example. Then ask your family what they can do to be good examples of people who are obedient. Finally, ask them to be extra attentive to the need to obey their parents, teachers, and anyone in authority over them—unless, of course, someone requests that they do something wrong.

Family Prayer

Saint Louis prescribes three prayers for today and throughout this phase of preparation. They are the Litany of the Holy Spirit, the Litany of the Blessed Virgin, and the Ave Maris Stella. You will find them in the appendix "Prayers for Consecration Preparation."
Find time today to pray the holy Rosary.

Evening

Day is done. It's time to pause for a moment to ponder your day. Help and encourage your family members to do so as well and to ask forgiveness for any shortcomings. Lovingly point out any areas in which better efforts are in order for the future. Always praise them for trying their best!

Continue to work on knowledge of self during this distinctive time as you strive to prepare for your consecration.

Bless your family with holy water before going to bed. Send everyone to bed with hugs and kisses, emphasizing that they are loved! Remind them to pray to their guardian angels.

Mary, My Mother

Dearest Mary, my Mother, thank you for your loving example of holy obedience. Teach me to be like you. I know I require a deeper humility. Please help me. Please also gather up all of my efforts today, as poor as they may be, and transform them into a fragrant bouquet for your dear Son. *Hail Mary . . .*

Day 15

Repent and Die to Self

Every day, from one end of the earth to the other, in
the highest heaven and in the lowest abyss, all things
preach, all things proclaim the wondrous Virgin Mary.
The nine choirs of angels, men and women of every
age, rank, and religion, both good and evil, even the
very devils themselves are compelled by the force of
truth, willingly or unwillingly, to call her blessed.[36]

—Saint Louis Marie de Montfort

---

[36] *True Devotion*, no. 8.

Family Consecration to Jesus through Mary

Morning

Raise your heart and mind to God. Put yourself in His presence. Pray your Morning Offering and the following prayer:

Dear Lord Jesus, morning is here and I thank you for caring for my family through the night and for gifting me with a brand-new day. Dear Mother Mary, help me to be attentive to serving lovingly those God calls me to serve: my family and my neighbor. Help me to learn from you. I entrust my day to your care. Dear Saint Joseph, you are my steady guide. Thank you. Amen.

Teaching for Parents

Saint Louis teaches us today about repenting of our sins and dying to ourselves.

Repent or Perish

At that very time there were some present who told him about the Galileans whose blood Pilate had mingled with their sacrifices. He asked them, "Do you think that because these Galileans suffered in this way they were worse sinners than all other Galileans? No, I tell you; but unless you repent, you will all perish as they did. Or those eighteen who were killed when the tower of Siloam fell on them—do you think that they were worse offenders than all the others living in Jerusalem? No, I tell you; but unless you repent, you will all perish just as they did." (Luke 13:1–5)

Dying to Ourselves Daily

In order to empty ourselves of self, we must die daily to ourselves. This involves our renouncing what the powers of the soul and the senses of the body incline us to do. We must see as if we did not see, hear as if we did not hear and use the things of this world as if we did not use them. This is what St. Paul calls "dying daily." Unless the grain of wheat falls to the ground and dies, it remains only a single grain and does not bear any good fruit. If we do not die to self and if our holiest devotions do not lead us to this necessary and fruitful death, we shall not bear fruit of any worth and our devotions will cease to be profitable. All our good works will be tainted by self-love and self-will so that our greatest sacrifices and our best actions will be unacceptable to God.

Consequently when we come to die we shall find ourselves devoid of virtue and merit and discover that we do not possess even one spark of that pure love which God shares only with those who have died to themselves and whose life is hidden with Jesus Christ in him.

We must choose among all the devotions to the Blessed Virgin the one which will lead us more surely to this dying to self.[37]

Teaching for Children

Today's teachings speak soberingly about the essential need for repentance and dying to self. These important teachings go directly against the messages of our worldly culture, which encourages us to put ourselves above others and seek to pursue what is ungodly.

---

[37] Saint Louis Marie de Montfort, *True Devotion*, nos. 81, 82.

Family Consecration to Jesus through Mary

To lead Christian lives, we must indeed be countercultural. We are living *in* the world, but we should not be *of* the world.

This reminds me so much of Venerable Archbishop Fulton Sheen's statements. He explained that it was easy to be Christian in the past. He said, "The atmosphere was Christian; morals were Christian; there was no great problem in adapting ourselves to a Christian society." He continued, "Today the current is against us. And today the mood of the world is, 'Go with the world, go with the spirit.'" I absolutely love what he said next. "Listen, dead bodies float downstream. Only live bodies resist the current. And so the good Lord is testing us."[38]

We absolutely need to be *live* bodies—full of a vibrant faith! Teach your children today that the world does not support our Catholic beliefs. Perhaps, at times it feels extremely difficult to be different, or perhaps we feel lonely not to fit in with some of our friends. Yet we should rejoice and be glad! We know that God is calling us to live the truth and be a shining, holy example of His love. We cannot go with the flow of society. We must be live bodies and must resist the current with God's amazing grace, with Mother Mary's help, and through our continual prayers.

Carry Out

When gathered together today at the dinner table, give your family three examples of situations in which your decisions to choose what is right might be difficult to do but will be pleasing to God and a striking example to others. Encourage your family to give at least one or two examples.

---

[38] Quoted in, "Archbishop Sheen's Warning of a Crisis in Christendom," *National Catholic Register*, http://www.ncregister.com/blog/joseph-pronechen/fulton-sheen-answers-for-a-christendom-crisis.

Family Prayer

Saint Louis prescribes three prayers for today and throughout this phase of preparation. They are the Litany of the Holy Spirit, the Litany of the Blessed Virgin, and the Ave Maris Stella. You will find them in the appendix "Prayers for Consecration Preparation."
Find time today to pray the holy Rosary.

Evening

Another day has come to an end. It's time to ponder the events and encounters of the day and to ask forgiveness for any shortcomings. Help your children to recount their day. Remember that during this week of preparation, you should earnestly strive to prepare your heart for your consecration and pray that you will recognize and discover knowledge of yourself. Always ask God for the graces to do so.

End the evening on a positive note, and offer inspiring and uplifting words or stories, lots of warm hugs, and good-night kisses. Let everyone know that they are loved! Let them know too, that their guardian angels are with them to protect them!

Mary, My Mother

Dearest Mary, my Mother, thank you for being with me this day as I have tried to walk forward in faith during my preparation to make my consecration to your Son, Jesus, through your loving hands and Immaculate Heart. We pray that we may learn to imitate your humble ways and to be more like your Son, Jesus. *Hail Mary . . .*

Day 16

Depend on God

The Mother of fair love will rid your heart of all scruples and inordinate servile fear. She will open and enlarge it to obey the commandments of her Son with alacrity and with the holy freedom of the children of God. She will fill your heart with pure love, of which she is the treasury. You will then cease to act as you did before, out of fear of the God who is love, but rather out of pure love."[39]

—Saint Louis Marie de Montfort

---

[39] *True Devotion*, no. 215.

Family Consecration to Jesus through Mary

Morning

Raise your heart and mind to God. Put yourself in His presence. Pray your Morning Offering and the following prayer:

Dear Lord Jesus, thank You for loving me. Help me to try my hardest to become a saint. Dear Mother Mary, help me humbly to open my ears to listen to Your Son, Jesus. You told the wine stewards at the wedding feast at Cana, "Do whatever He tells you." I want to do what Jesus wants. I also ask you to help me to obtain the grace of self-knowledge. I entrust my day to your care. Dear Saint Joseph, be my guide today. Amen.

Teaching for Parents

Today, we learn more about the need for humility and about knowing oneself.

Striving for Self-Knowledge

During the first week they should offer up all their prayers and acts of devotion to acquire knowledge of themselves and sorrow for their sins.

Let them perform all their actions in a spirit of humility. With this end in view, they may, if they wish, meditate on what I have said concerning our corrupted nature, and consider themselves during six days of the week as nothing but snails, slugs, toads, swine, snakes, and goats. Or else they may meditate on the following three considerations of St. Bernard: "Remember what you were—corrupted seed; what you are—a body destined for decay; what you will be—food for worms."

They will ask our Lord and the Holy Spirit to enlighten them saying, "Lord, that I may see," or "Lord, let me know myself," or the "Come, Holy Spirit." Every day they should say the Litany of the Holy Spirit, with the prayer that follows, as indicated in the first part of this work. They will turn to our Blessed Lady and beg her to obtain for them that great grace which is the foundation of all others, the grace of self-knowledge. For this intention they will say each day the Ave Maris Stella and the Litany of the Blessed Virgin.[40]

Our Blindness to Ourselves

We must not rely too much upon ourselves, for grace and understanding are often lacking in us. We have but little inborn light, and this we quickly lose through negligence. Often we are not aware that we are so blind in heart. Meanwhile we do wrong, and then do worse in excusing it. At times we are moved by passion, and we think it zeal. We take others to task for small mistakes, and overlook greater ones in ourselves. We are quick enough to feel and brood over the things we suffer from others, but we think nothing of how much others suffer from us. If a man would weigh his own deeds fully and rightly, he would find little cause to pass severe judgment on others.[41]

Teaching for Children

The readings today are about self-knowledge and the need to be sorry for our sins. The verse from Saint Louis that begins our reflection today instructs us that Mary "will fill your heart with pure

---

[40] Saint Louis Marie de Montfort, *True Devotion*, no. 228.
[41] Thomas à Kempis, *Imitation*, bk. 2, chap. 5.

love of which she is the treasury. You will then cease to act as you did before, out of fear of the God who is love, but rather out of pure love." Thus, we come to understand that we must obey the commandments, learn to perform our acts with humility, refrain from passing judgment on others, and realize that we are nothing at all without God.

As Saint Louis pointed out, St. Bernard said, "Remember what you were — corrupted seed; what you are — a body destined for decay; what you will be — food for worms." While that might be a bit tough to explain to your children, tell them that we need to depend on God for everything. He made us, and we need to listen to Him and to stay on the right path — always! Pray about a way that you can impress today's teachings on your children's hearts. Perhaps, you will use a personal story about when you might have chosen the wrong way or when you almost did and how you came to realize that God's way is the only way.

Carry Out

When gathered together today, ask your family members how we can show God that we love Him — and do so out of pure love, not because we are afraid of Him. I think you might be surprised by the responses from your children. Ask them to carry out their works of love soon.

Family Prayer

Saint Louis prescribes three prayers for today and throughout this phase of preparation. They are the Litany of the Holy Spirit, the Litany of the Blessed Virgin, and the Ave Maris Stella. You will find them in the appendix "Prayers for Consecration Preparation."

Find time today to pray the holy Rosary.

Evening

As evening falls, take a few moments to ponder the events of your day. Ask forgiveness for your shortcomings and for grace to do a better job tomorrow. Call upon the saints and the holy angels to be with you and your family this evening. Resolve to focus on holiness tomorrow and to spend less time on secular activities to allow for quiet time for prayer and pondering. Be earnest in your consecration preparation.

Be sure to instill a healthy dose of peace and happiness in your family's hearts at bedtime. Bless the family with holy water before going to bed. End the evening with inspiring and uplifting words or stories, lots of warm hugs, and good-night kisses. Let everyone know that they are loved!

Mary, My Mother

Dearest Mary, my Mother, thank you for being with me this day as I have tried to walk forward in faith during my preparation to make my consecration to your Son, Jesus, through your loving hands and Immaculate Heart. Please help me to become truly humble and to obtain the grace of self- knowledge as I progress this week. *Hail Mary . . .*

Day 17

Be a Good Steward

Mary, Star of the sea, guides all her faithful servants into safe harbor. She shows them the path to eternal life and helps them avoid dangerous pitfalls. She leads them by the hand along the path of holiness, steadies them when they are liable to fall, and helps them rise when they have fallen. She chides them like a loving mother when they are remiss, and sometimes she even lovingly chastises them. How could a child who follows such a mother and such an enlightened guide as Mary take the wrong path to Heaven? Follow her and you cannot go wrong, says Saint Bernard. There is no danger of a true child of Mary being led astray by the devil and falling into heresy. Where Mary leads, Satan with his deceptions and heretics with their subtleties are not encountered. "When she upholds you, you will not fall."[42]

—Saint Louis Marie de Montfort

---

[42] *True Devotion*, no. 209.

Family Consecration to Jesus through Mary

Morning

Raise your heart and mind to God. Put yourself in His presence. Pray your Morning Offering and the following prayer:

Dear Lord Jesus, thank You for caring for my family through the night and gifting me with a brand-new day. Defend me from all evil. Help me to live our day well—humbly striving to transform my heart. Dear Mother Mary, help me to be attentive to the needs around me, starting with my family. I entrust my day to your care. Dear Saint Joseph, please protect my family. Amen.

Teaching for Parents

The readings today focus on sin and its consquences and on divine judgment.

Judgment and the Punishment of Sin

In all things, consider the end; how you shall stand before the strict Judge from whom nothing is hidden and who will pronounce judgment in all justice, accepting neither bribes nor excuses. And you, miserable and wretched sinner, who fear even the countenance of an angry man, what answer will you make to the God who knows all your sins? Why do you not provide for yourself against the day of judgment when no man can be excused or defended by another because each will have enough to do to answer for himself?[43]

---

[43] Thomas à Kempis, *Imitation*, bk. 1, chap. 24.

The Parable of the Dishonest Manager

Then Jesus said to the disciples, "There was a rich man who had a manager, and charges were brought to him that this man was squandering his property. So he summoned him and said to him, 'What is this that I hear about you? Give me an accounting of your management, because you cannot be my manager any longer.' Then the manager said to himself, 'What will I do, now that my master is taking the position away from me? I am not strong enough to dig, and I am ashamed to beg. I have decided what to do so that, when I am dismissed as manager, people may welcome me into their homes.' So, summoning his master's debtors one by one, he asked the first, 'How much do you owe my master?' He answered, 'A hundred jugs of olive oil.' He said to him, 'Take your bill, sit down quickly, and make it fifty.' Then he asked another, 'And how much do you owe?' He replied, 'A hundred containers of wheat.' He said to him, 'Take your bill and make it eighty.' And his master commended the dishonest manager because he had acted shrewdly; for the children of this age are more shrewd in dealing with their own generation than are the children of light." (Luke 16:1–8)

Teaching for Children

In today's first reading, we learn that we will face the just Judge one day and are responsible for our own lives. At that point, no one will be able to stand up for us or to make excuses for lives that were not lived well. The second teaching, "The Parable of the Dishonest Manager," might be a tough parable to understand. We may wonder why it would seem that Jesus is pleased with a dishonest manager. Perhaps we should ponder the fact that Jesus is telling us that we can learn even from the dishonest. The manager was faced with a crisis when losing his job, and he was quick to think on his feet. Perhaps he tried to rectify the problem by making friends with his master's debtors, possibly forgoing his commission in an attempt to make things right.

We can ask ourselves what kind of stewards we are with the gifts God has given us. Do we squander our God-given gifts? Have we given enough away to the needy?

As well, we read in our verse today that Mary, Star of the Sea, "guides all her faithful servants into safe harbor. She shows them the path to eternal life and helps them avoid dangerous pitfalls." This reminds me of Saint Faustina, who said that she visited Purgatory at the command of God and she saw the suffering souls there who were comforted by the Blessed Mother, whom they called the "Star of the Sea."

Teach your children that we should always stay close to Mother Mary, the Star of the Sea, who will unfailingly guide us to safety. If we follow the commandments and listen to our Mother in Heaven, we will not fall into the devil's traps. Let your children know that we can call on Mary at any time. She will come to our rescue.

Carry Out

Sometime today, gather your children (perhaps keep them at the dinner table a few minutes longer). Pray the Hail Mary slowly together. If desired, provide paper and crayons or markers and draw pictures of Mary, Star of the Sea, guiding and protecting her children.

Family Prayer

Saint Louis prescribes three prayers for today and throughout this phase of preparation. They are the Litany of the Holy Spirit, the

Litany of the Blessed Virgin, and the Ave Maris Stella. You will find them in the appendix "Prayers for Consecration Preparation." *Find time today to pray the holy Rosary.*

Evening

Evening is here. It's time to ponder the events and encounters of the day and to ask forgiveness for any shortcomings. Thank God for the blessing of a new day tomorrow to move forward once again. Strive to focus on the teachings provided and spend less time on anything that will distract you from focusing on this special consecration preparation.

Ending the day on a positive note, offer happy and inspiring stories, lots of warm hugs, and good-night kisses. Let everyone know that they are loved! Let them know, too, that their guardian angels are with them to protect them!

Mary, My Mother

Dearest Mary, my Mother, thank you for being with me this day. I need you. You are my Star of the Sea, my sure guide to your Son, Jesus. Please continue to take me through this preparation, and grant me the graces to do a good job tomorrow. Help me to be humble. Also, please place your protective mantle around me to protect me as I sleep. *Hail Mary . . .*

Day 18

Lead an Honest and Holy Life

Mary, the beloved Mother of chosen souls, shelters them under her protecting wings as a hen does her chicks. She speaks to them, coming down to their level and accommodating herself to all their weaknesses. To ensure their safety from the hawk and vulture, she becomes their escort, surrounding them as an army in battle array. Could anyone surrounded by a well-ordered army of, say, a hundred thousand men fear his enemies? No, and still less would a faithful servant of Mary, protected on all sides by her imperial forces, fear his enemy. This powerful Queen of Heaven would sooner dispatch millions of angels to help one of her servants than have it said that a single faithful and trusting servant of hers had fallen victim to the malice, number, and power of his enemies.[44]

—Saint Louis Marie de Montfort

[44] *True Devotion*, no. 210.

Morning

Raise your heart and mind to God. Put yourself in His presence. Pray your Morning Offering and the following prayer:

Dear Lord Jesus, thank you for a fresh new morning. Help me to live today for You. Dear Mother Mary, help me humbly to prepare my mind, heart, and soul for my upcoming consecration to your Son, Jesus, through your sweet hands and Immaculate Heart. I humbly hand over my day to your care. Dear Saint Joseph, please watch over me today. Amen.

Teaching for Parents

Today. we learn about the danger of leading others astray, the need to correct others, the power of faith, and humble service.

On Leading Others Astray

Jesus said to his disciples, "Occasions for stumbling are bound to come, but woe to anyone by whom they come! It would be better for you if a millstone were hung around your neck and you were thrown into the sea than for you to cause one of these little ones to stumble. Be on your guard!" (Luke 17:1–3)

Brotherly Correction

"If another disciple sins, you must rebuke the offender, and if there is repentance, you must forgive. And if the same person sins against you seven times a day, and turns back to you seven times and says, 'I repent,' you must forgive." (Luke 17:3–4)

The Power of Faith

The apostles said to the Lord, "Increase our faith!" The Lord replied, "If you had faith the size of a mustard seed, you could say to this mulberry tree, 'Be uprooted and planted in the sea,' and it would obey you." (Luke 17:5–6)

Humble Service

"Who among you would say to your slave who has just come in from plowing or tending sheep in the field, 'Come here at once and take your place at the table'? Would you not rather say to him, 'Prepare supper for me, put on your apron and serve me while I eat and drink; later you may eat and drink'? Do you thank the slave for doing what was commanded? So you also, when you have done all that you were ordered to do, say, 'We are worthless slaves; we have done only what we ought to have done!'" (Luke 17:7–10)

All Grievous Things Are to Be Endured to Life Everlasting

The voice of Christ:

My child, do not let the labors which you have taken up for My sake break you, and do not let troubles, from whatever source, cast you down; but in everything let My promise strengthen and console you. I am able to reward you beyond all means and measure.

You will not labor here long, nor will you always be oppressed by sorrows. Wait a little while, and you will see a speedy end of evils. The hour will come when all labor and trouble shall be no more. All that passes away with time is trivial.[45]

---

[45] Thomas à Kempis, *Imitation*, bk. 3, chap. 47.

Family Consecration to Jesus through Mary

Teaching for Children

Today our teachings speak about the consequences of leading others astray and about brotherly correction, the power of faith, humble service, and the difficulty of denying ourselves, picking up our crosses, and following Jesus. Jesus tells us, however, that the sorrows and difficulties in this life will come to an end. He also promises to strengthen us and to console us.

Talk to your children about the need to lead honest, holy lives. Explain that every single day is filled with many choices. Will we choose the good, or will we choose the bad? Will we lead others astray by our words or actions? Or will we set holy examples and inspire others to choose what is right? Emphasize that not everyone is happy when others do good. They might be jealous, or for some reason, they might choose to do evil. They might poke fun at us. This is not a reason to change our ways, for we want to serve God and please Him, not be concerned about pleasing others, especially when it is contrary to our beliefs.

Remind your children that just as you always protect them from harm, Mother Mary will guide and protect her children in the spiritual life like an army in battle array, as we read in Saint Louis de Montfort's words that begin our reflection today. Turn to Mother Mary often.

Carry Out

Take a look at the appendix "Interior and Exterior Practices." Choose one or two items that your family can carry out today or sometime soon. As well, when gathered at the table today, ask your family to list three ways in which they can be shining examples of Christians in action or three ways they can help someone to learn about the Blessed Mother.

Family Prayer

Saint Louis prescribes three prayers for today and throughout this phase of preparation. They are the Litany of the Holy Spirit, the Litany of the Blessed Virgin, and the Ave Maris Stella. You will find them in the appendix "Prayers for Consecration Preparation."
Find time today to pray the holy Rosary.

Evening

It's time to take a few moments to ponder the day and ask forgiveness for any shortcomings. Tomorrow will soon be here—another opportunity to strive for holiness once again. Throughout this distinctive preparatory time, strive to focus on holiness and spend less time on the secular so that you will have the opportunities to reflect on self-knowledge.

Always tuck the family in bed after inspiring and uplifting words or stories, with lots of warm hugs and good-night kisses. Let everyone know that they are loved! Remind them that holy angels are all around!

Mary, My Mother

Dearest Mary, my Mother, thank you for being with me this day, guiding me and protecting me like an army in battle array while I prepare to make my Marian consecration. Please gather up all of my efforts today and transform them into a fragrant bouquet for your dear Son.
Hail Mary . . .

Day 19

Have a Childlike Heart

How welcome to Jesus Christ, the Father of the world to come, is a child perfumed with the fragrance of Mary! How readily and how intimately does he unite himself to that child!... Furthermore, once Mary has heaped her favors upon her children and her faithful servants and has secured for them the blessing of the heavenly Father and union with Jesus Christ, she keeps them in Jesus and keeps Jesus in them. She guards them, watching over them unceasingly, lest they lose the grace of God and fall into the snares of their enemies. "She keeps the saints in their fullness" (Saint Bonaventure) and inspires them to persevere to the end.[46]

—Saint Louis Marie de Montfort

[46] *True Devotion*, nos. 211–212.

Family Consecration to Jesus through Mary

Morning

Raise your heart and mind to God. Put yourself in His presence. Pray your Morning Offering and the following prayer:

Dear Lord Jesus, we arise afresh with this new morning. I am thankful for Your loving care. Please guide my family to prepare our hearts to make a worthy and beautiful consecration to You. Dear Mother Mary, thank you for being my Mother. Teach me and help me to be a beautiful and humble child of God. I desire to be perfumed with your fragrance! I respectfully entrust my day to you. Dear Saint Joseph, please pray for me. Amen.

Teaching for Parents

Today's readings teach us about the need to be humble like children in order to enter the Kingdom of God. We are reminded about the dangers of riches and materialism.

Jesus Blesses Little Children

People were bringing even infants to him that he might touch them; and when the disciples saw it, they sternly ordered them not to do it. But Jesus called for them and said, "Let the little children come to me, and do not stop them; for it is to such as these that the kingdom of God belongs. Truly I tell you, whoever does not receive the kingdom of God as a little child will never enter it." (Luke 18:15–17)

The Danger of Riches

A certain ruler asked him, "Good Teacher, what must I do to inherit eternal life?" Jesus said to him, "Why do you call me good? No one is good but God alone. You know the commandments: 'You shall not commit adultery; You shall not murder; You shall not steal; You shall not bear false witness; Honor your father and mother.'" He replied, "I have kept all these since my youth." (Luke 18:18–21)

When Jesus heard this, he said to him, "There is still one thing lacking. Sell all that you own and distribute the money to the poor, and you will have treasure in heaven; then come, follow me." But when he heard this, he became sad; for he was very rich. Jesus looked at him and said, "How hard it is for those who have wealth to enter the kingdom of God! Indeed, it is easier for a camel to go through the eye of a needle than for someone who is rich to enter the kingdom of God."

Those who heard it said, "Then who can be saved?" He replied, "What is impossible for mortals is possible for God." (Luke 18:22–27)

The Reward of Renunciation

Then Peter said, "Look, we have left our homes and followed you." And he said to them, "Truly I tell you, there is no one who has left house or wife or brothers or parents or children, for the sake of the kingdom of God, who will not get back very much more in this age, and in the age to come eternal life." (Luke 18:27–30)

Family Consecration to Jesus through Mary

Teaching for Children

We learn today about the gift of children and that Jesus desires that they come to Him. And, further, He says, "Whoever does not receive the kingdom of God as a little child will never enter it." We read about the danger of riches and the reward of renunciation.

Explain the parable about the danger of riches to your children. Talk to them about the need to be unattached to material things. It's okay to like things, but we can never allow them to become our "god." That is a real danger in a world that beckons us to become materialistic. As well, impress upon your children that God expects that we will help others who are in need. He gives to us and asks us to give to the unfortunate. I can't help but think of dear Mother Teresa of Calcutta, who saw Jesus in everyone she served. She wholeheartedly followed Jesus' words in Matthew's Gospel: "Truly I tell you, just as you did it to one of the least of these who are members of my family, you did it to me" (Matt. 25:40). Teach your children that Our Lord instructs us to care for others, not to store up riches for ourselves. As well, they should retain their childlike innocent hearts.

Finally, impress upon your children the need to stay close to Mother Mary. We read in the verse from Saint Louis that begins our day that Mary perfumes us with her "fragrance"! She takes care of us and gets us ready for her Son, Jesus. Mary keeps us safe!

Carry Out

Ask your family to consider a selfless (possibly anonymous) Marian work of mercy that they can carry out. What will it be? Discuss it at the family table and jot down a few ideas. Do your best to carry it out soon.

Family Prayer

Saint Louis prescribes three prayers for today and throughout this phase of preparation. They are the Litany of the Holy Spirit, the Litany of the Blessed Virgin, and the Ave Maris Stella. You will find them in the appendix "Prayers for Consecration Preparation." *Find time today to pray the holy Rosary.*

Evening

Settle into a peaceful evening. Encourage your family members to take a few moments to ponder the day and ask forgiveness for any shortcomings and express thanks for the blessing of a new day tomorrow to strive for holiness once again. Help your little ones with this.

Once again tomorrow, you can focus on holiness and spend less time on the secular during this time of preparation. End the evening with inspiring and uplifting words or stories, lots of warm hugs, and good-night kisses. Let everyone know that they are loved!

Mary, My Mother

Dearest Mary, my Mother, thank you for the gift of you. Continue to help my family to prepare for our consecration to your Son, Jesus, through your loving hands and Immaculate heart. Please gather up all of my earnest efforts from today and transform them into a beautiful bouquet exuding your heavenly fragrance, and please present it to your dear Son on my behalf. *Hail Mary . . .*

Family Activity for Part 2

Sing a Song to Mary!

It is said that to sing is to pray twice. Sometime very soon, perhaps on a Sunday, gather together and jot down some attributes of Mother Mary. Help your children with this. Perhaps, look at the Litany of the Blessed Virgin in the appendix of additional prayers in the back of this book. After you come up with attributes and, hopefully, additional feedback from your children, compose a song to Mary! Don't be afraid — you can do it! You don't have to have a music degree or masterful voices — just a heart for Mary.

An alternative idea is to find a beautiful hymn to Mary and sing it together at home — your domestic church. Consider singing it every day for the remainder of your preparation. Saint Faustina's father, Stanislaus Kowalska, used to sing hymns to Mary very loudly every morning. It made an impact on his family. Sing to Mary!

Part 3

Obtaining Knowledge of
the Blessed Virgin

Mary embraces God's will and freely chooses to
cooperate with God's grace, thereby fulfilling a
crucial role in God's plan of salvation. Throughout
the centuries, the Church has turned to the
Blessed Virgin in order to come closer to Christ.
Many forms of piety toward the Mother of God
developed that help bring us closer to her Son.

—United States Conference of Catholic Bishops, "Mary"

We begin part 3 of our preparation, which is knowledge of Mary.
Saint Louis de Montfort proclaimed that the ten principal virtues of
Mary are: "her profound humility, her lively faith, her blind obedience, her continual mental prayer, her mortification in all things,
her surpassing purity, her ardent charity, her heroic patience, her
angelic sweetness, and her divine wisdom."[47]

[47] Saint Louis Marie de Montfort, *Preparation for Total Consecration*, 37.

Family Consecration to Jesus through Mary

This Marian saint instructs us that we must unite ourselves to Jesus through Mary. That is precisely what we are working to accomplish through this preparation and subsequent consecration. In order to do so, we should become familiar with the Blessed Virgin Mary, our dear Mother and Mediatrix. We will learn more this week by studying the interior life of Mary, her virtues, her participation in her Son's mission, and her union with Him. Try hard to dig in prayerfully this week. Make every day count.

Day 20

Ponder Jesus' Birth and Boyhood

Your lives must be like mine: quiet and
hidden, in unceasing union with God,
pleading for humanity and preparing the
world for the second coming of God.[48]

—Our Blessed Mother to Saint Faustina

---

[48] Saint Maria Faustina Kowalska, *Diary*, no. 625.

Family Consecration to Jesus through Mary

Teaching for Parents

Today's readings are on Jesus' birth and boyhood.

The Adoration of the Shepherds

So they went with haste and found Mary and Joseph, and the
child lying in the manger. When they saw this, they made
known what had been told them about this child; and all who
heard it were amazed at what the shepherds told them. But
Mary treasured all these words and pondered them in her heart.
The shepherds returned, glorifying and praising God for all they
had heard and seen, as it had been told them. (Luke 2:16–20)

Jesus Is Named

After eight days had passed, it was time to circumcise the
child; and he was called Jesus, the name given by the angel
before he was conceived in the womb. (Luke 2:21)

The Boy Jesus in the Temple

Now every year his parents went to Jerusalem for the festival of the Passover. And when he was twelve years old, they went up as usual for the festival. When the festival was ended and they started to return, the boy Jesus stayed behind in Jerusalem, but his parents did not know it. Assuming that he was in the group of travelers, they went a day's journey. Then they started to look for him among their relatives and friends. When they did not find him, they returned to Jerusalem to search for him. After three days they found him in the temple, sitting among the teachers, listening to them and asking them questions. And all who heard him were amazed at his understanding and his answers. When his parents saw him they were astonished; and his mother said to him, "Child, why have you treated us like this? Look, your father and I have been searching for you in great anxiety." He said to them, "Why were you searching for me? Did you not know that I must be in my Father's house?" But they did not understand what he said to them. Then he went down with them and came to Nazareth, and was obedient to them. His mother treasured all these things in her heart.

And Jesus increased in wisdom and in years, and in divine and human favor. (Luke 2:41–52)

Teaching for Children

In today's teachings we are reminded of Jesus' birth, His being named and circumcised, and His being lost in the Temple as a boy. Read and explain today's readings to your children. You might ask a few questions:

- What do you think it was like to be a shepherd and to find Mary, Joseph, and Baby Jesus lying in a manger?
- Isn't it amazing that Baby Jesus was born in a simple manger meant for animals, even though He was God? You can tell your children that He teaches us that we should all be humble and poor in spirit.
- How do you think Mary and Joseph felt when they couldn't find their Son, Jesus? Why was Jesus talking to the men in the Temple?

Explain that Jesus did what God the Father had called Him to do. After that, He went home with Mary and Joseph and was obedient to them. Mary trusted in God's providence. She lived in the present and knew that all of these moments were special, including everything that led up to these moments, and she treasured them all in her heart. We, too, can treasure these teachings and our Catholic Faith.

Carry Out

Ask your family to be extra attentive to the teachings and prayer today. Remind them that Mother Mary is with you all, helping you to prepare for your upcoming consecration. Get to know her more through your prayers to her and through study.

Family Prayer

Saint Louis prescribes four prayers for today and throughout this phase of preparation. They are the Litany of the Holy Spirit, the Litany of the Blessed Virgin, the Ave Maris Stella, and Saint Louis de Montfort's Prayer to Mary. You can find them in the appendix "Prayers for Consecration Preparation."

Find time today to pray the holy Rosary.

Evening

It's time to settle down for the evening. Endeavor to place all of your concerns and weariness of the day into the hands of Mother Mary. During bedtime prayers, encourage everyone to ponder the day, to ask forgiveness for any shortcomings, and to express thanks for the blessings of today.

Bless your family with holy water and pray the prayer to Mary (below). Remind your family that they can call upon Jesus, Mary, the saints, and their guardian angels at any time of the day or night.

Mary, My Mother

Dearest Mary, my Mother, thank you for being with me today. Help me to treasure my life—each moment. Teach me throughout this week. I desire to learn much more about you and your Son, Jesus. Please bless my efforts as only you can and envelop them in your holy perfume to be presented to your Son, Jesus. Please give me a restful night. *Hail Mary . . .*

Day 21

Get Close to Mother Mary

Go to the Madonna. Love her! Always say
the Rosary. Say it well. Say it as often as you
can! Be souls of prayer. Never tire of praying,
it is what is essential. Prayer shakes the Heart
of God, it obtains necessary graces!"[49]

—Saint Padre Pio

---

[49] Quoted in Amanda Evinger, "How I Learned to Stop Worrying and Pray the Rosary," *National Catholic Register*, https://www.ncregister.com/blog/evinger/how-i-learned-to-stop-worrying-and-love-the-rosary.

Family Consecration to Jesus through Mary

Morning

Raise your heart and mind to God. Put yourself in His presence. Pray your Morning Offering and the following prayer:

Dear Lord Jesus, thank You for the gift of a new day to praise and glorify You and learn about Your holy Mother. Dear Mother Mary, I want to learn to turn to you continually throughout my days. I want to be more faithful to my prayers and never tire of doing good and helping others to get to Heaven by my holy life and example. I entrust my day to your motherly care. Amen.

Teaching for Parents

Today we focus on devotion to the Blessed Mother and ultimately how close we desire to be to her.

Kinds of Devotion to the Blessed Virgin Mary

If we would go up to God, and be united with Him, we must use the same means He used to come down to us to be made Man and to impart His graces to us. This means is a true devotion to our Blessed Lady. There are several true devotions to our Lady: here I do not speak of those which are false. The first consists in fulfilling our Christian duties, avoiding mortal sin, acting more out of love than with fear, praying to our Lady now and then, honoring her as the Mother of God, yet without having any special devotion to her. The second consists in entertaining for Our Lady more perfect feelings of esteem and love, of confidence and veneration. It leads us to join the Confraternities of the Holy Rosary and of the Scapular, to recite the five or the fifteen decades of the Holy Rosary, to honor Mary's images and altars, to publish her praises, and to enroll ourselves in her modalities. This devotion is good, holy, and praiseworthy if we keep ourselves free from sin. But it is not so perfect as the next, nor so efficient in severing our soul from creatures, in detaching ourselves in order to be united with Jesus Christ. The third devotion to Our Lady, known and practiced by very few persons, is this I am about to disclose to you, predestinate soul. It consists in giving oneself entirely and as a slave to Mary, and to Jesus through Mary, and after that, to do all that we do, through Mary, with Mary, in Mary, and for Mary. We should choose a special feast day on which we give, consecrate, and sacrifice to Mary voluntarily, lovingly, and without constraint, entirely and without reserve: our body and soul, our exterior property, such as house, family and income, and also our interior and spiritual possessions: namely, our merits, graces, virtues, and satisfactions.[50]

Teaching for Children

We learn today from Saint Louis that we ultimately choose how close we desire to get to Mary. While that might sound a bit funny, it is one way to explain the three ways that the Marian saint mapped out for us. Which one will we choose? Hopefully, it will be the third, which is the most perfect. Since you are preparing for your Marian consecration, you are already choosing the most perfect way.

Talk to your children about these three ways in which to be devoted to the Blessed Mother. Let them know that in choosing the very best and most perfect way, we are putting our very lives

---

[50] Saint Louis de Montfort, *The Secret of Mary*, nos. 23–24.

into our dear Mother's hands. The most pure Virgin Mary wants the absolute best for each one of her children. When we consecrate our lives to Jesus through Mary, we are ultimately trusting Mother Mary to help unite us to her Son and to work through us for God's glory. We give ourselves to Divine Love. Ask each of your family members which way they choose to be devoted to Mary.

Carry Out

Ask your children to suggest three ways they can show Mother Mary their love today. Help them with this and praise them for their responses. Encourage your family to pray an extra decade of the Rosary today out of their love for Our Lady.

Family Prayer

Saint Louis prescribes four prayers for today and throughout this phase of preparation. They are the Litany of the Holy Spirit, the Litany of the Blessed Virgin, the Ave Maris Stella, and Saint Louis de Montfort's Prayer to Mary. You can find them in the appendix "Prayers for Consecration Preparation."

Find time today to pray the holy Rosary.

Evening

This evening is yet another opportunity for everyone to turn to God and ask forgiveness for any shortcomings. If someone cannot think of any, ask family members to remind that individual (nicely!), and encourage all to offer any necessary forgiveness or sorrow—whatever the case may be. As well, rejoice over the goodness of the day. Take a moment to ponder the most meaningful parts.

Try your best to keep a peaceful, happy, holy atmosphere this evening. Bless everyone with holy water and tuck them into bed with love.

Mary, My Mother

Dearest Mary, my Mother, thank you for being with me this day as I have worked on my preparation to make my consecration to your Son, Jesus, through your loving hands and Immaculate Heart. Please gather up all of my prayers and efforts and transform them into a fragrant bouquet to give to your dear Son. *Hail Mary . . .*

Day 22

Strive for True Devotion to Our Lady

By her divine motherhood, Mary fully opened
her heart to Christ and, in Him, to all humanity.
Mary's total dedication to the work of her Son
is especially shown by her participation in His
sacrifice. According to John's testimony, the
Mother of Jesus "stood by the cross" (John 19:25).
She thus united herself to all the sufferings that
Jesus endured. She shared in the generous offering
of his sacrifice for the salvation of mankind.[51]

—Saint John Paul II

---

[51] General Audience, Wednesday, April 29, 1998.

Family Consecration to Jesus through Mary

Morning

Raise your heart and mind to God. Put yourself in His presence. Pray your Morning Offering and the following prayer:

Dear Lord Jesus, thank You for the gift of my family and a new day to work hard on my pilgrimage of holiness. Dear Mother Mary, you are my Mother and my glorious example to follow. You heroically suffered along with your Son. You teach me how to be dedicated to the Lord and to be present to those who suffer. I entrust my day to you. Dear Saint Joseph, please guide and protect my family. Amen.

Teaching for Parents

We learn from Saint Louis many aspects of devotion to the Blessed Virgin Mary.

The Characteristics of True Devotion

After having explained and condemned false devotions to the Blessed Virgin, we shall now briefly describe what true devotion is. It is interior, trustful, holy, constant, and disinterested.

First, true devotion to our Lady is interior, that is, it comes from within the mind and the heart and follows from the esteem in which we hold her, the high regard we have for her greatness, and the love we bear her.

Second, it is trustful, that is to say, it fills us with confidence in the Blessed Virgin, the confidence that a child has for its loving Mother. It prompts us to go to her in every need of body and soul with great simplicity, trust, and affection. We implore our Mother's help always, everywhere, and for everything. We pray to her to be enlightened in our doubts, to be put back on the right path when we go astray, to be protected when we are tempted, to be strengthened when we are weakening, to be lifted up when we fall into sin, to be encouraged when we are losing heart, to be rid of our scruples, to be consoled in the trials, crosses and disappointments of life. Finally, in all our afflictions of body and soul, we naturally turn to Mary for help, with never a fear of importuning her or displeasing our Lord.

Third, true devotion to our Lady is holy, that is, it leads us to avoid sin and to imitate the virtues of Mary. Her ten principal virtues are: deep humility, lively faith, blind obedience, unceasing prayer, constant self-denial, surpassing purity, ardent love, heroic patience, angelic kindness, and heavenly wisdom.

Fourth, true devotion to our Lady is constant. It strengthens us in our desire to do good and prevents us from giving up our devotional practices too easily. It gives us the courage to oppose the fashions and maxims of the world, the vexations and unruly inclinations of the flesh and the temptations of the devil. Thus, a person truly devoted to our Blessed Lady is not changeable, fretful, scrupulous, or timid. We do not say, however, that such a person never sins or that his sensible feelings of devotion never change. When he has fallen, he stretches out his hand to his Blessed Mother and rises again. If he loses all taste and feeling for devotion, he is not at all upset, because a good and faithful servant of Mary is guided in his life by faith in Jesus and Mary, and not by feelings.

Fifth, true devotion to Mary is disinterested. It inspires us to seek God alone in His Blessed Mother and not ourselves. The true subject of Mary does not serve his illustrious Queen for selfish gain. He does not serve her for temporal or eternal well-being but simply and solely because she has the right to be served and God alone in her.[52]

Teaching for Children

Saint Louis stated that true devotion to Our Lady is "interior, trustful, holy, constant, and disinterested." In this teaching from *True Devotion*, he breaks this apart and explains. Talk to the children about this.

Tell them that as they grow closer to Mother Mary with their prayers to her and their conversations with her, they will develop a beautiful interior devotion to her. Their love for her will grow. They should never hesitate to reach out to Mary.

Our love for Mary should be trustful. This is easier for children than for adults. Let the children know that Mary is truly their Mother in Heaven and that they can form a very intimate relationship with her in their prayers to her. Encourage them to speak to her often. Saint Louis tells us never to fear to ask Mary's help in any situation. Emphasize this in your own words. Give examples.

Having a true devotion to Mary (or developing one) helps us to avoid sin and become holy. Saint Louis encourages us to imitate Mary's virtues: deep humility, lively faith, blind obedience, unceasing prayer, constant self-denial, surpassing purity, ardent love, heroic patience, angelic kindness, and heavenly wisdom. Give your children some examples of how they can imitate Mary's virtues.

Saint Louis teaches us that our true devotion to Mary will help us to be steady—will help us to stay the course. If we fall, with Mary's help we get up, dust ourselves off, and continue to walk in faith. Saint Louis also instructs us that even if we don't "feel" very

[52] Saint Louis Marie de Montfort, *True Devotion*, nos. 105–110.

well in our spiritual lives, we should continue on the right path and trust Jesus and Mary—not our feelings. Encourage your children, however, always to feel comfortable in expressing their feelings to you. You can then help them to sort them out.

Saint Louis teaches that true devotion to Mary also means that we love and trust her wholeheartedly and for the right reasons, which are never selfish. We can ask Mother Mary for the graces to "seek God alone in his Blessed Mother and not ourselves."

Carry Out

In our verse above, Saint John Paul II points out that according to John's testimony, Mary "stood by the cross" of her Son (John 19:25). As you and your family ponder the teachings of Saint Louis today on what it is to have "true devotion" to the Blessed Mother, consider also the sorrowful time that she spent at the foot of her Son's Cross. No doubt, Mary suffered intensely watching and waiting—observing every drop of precious blood that fell to the ground from her Son's body and hearing His sighs of agony.

Mary teaches us to stand by the foot of the Cross in our own lives—to be present to those in need of comfort. Think of someone you know who needs comfort right now. Talk to your family about a work of mercy you can soon do for that person. Be like Mary.

Family Prayer

Saint Louis prescribes four prayers for today and throughout this phase of preparation. They are the Litany of the Holy Spirit, the Litany of the Blessed Virgin, the Ave Maris Stella, and Saint Louis de Montfort's Prayer to Mary. You can find them in the appendix "Prayers for Consecration Preparation."

Find time today to pray the holy Rosary.

Family Consecration to Jesus through Mary

Evening

As evening falls, try your best to foster a calm atmosphere. If arguments or discord erupts, nip it in the bud. Replace it with calming words and prayers. Praise your family for their loving efforts in staying the course in their family consecration preparation thus far. Give them encouragement to keep going—one foot in front of the other each day as they walk in faith, mindful that the evil one tries to stop you from continuing on. Move forward with love, conviction, and courage. Pray for the graces! Begin anew tomorrow. After prayers and blessings, rest well tonight with holy angels all around!

Mary, My Mother

O Immaculata, my Mother, thank you for guiding me this day during my preparation to make my consecration to your Son, Jesus, through your loving hands and Immaculate Heart. Please gather up all of my efforts today, as poor as they may be, and transform them into little precious gems for your dear Son. Please keep me under your protective mantle tonight. *Hail Mary* . . .

Day 23

Learn the Elements of Marian Consecration

Come, my Beloved, my Spouse, come
to my temple. Where I wish to hear thy
voice of praise and worship."[53]

—The Most High God to the Blessed Virgin when
she entered the Temple at three years old

[53] Venerable Mary of Agreda, *Mystical City of God*, chap. 1.

Family Consecration to Jesus through Mary

Morning

Raise your heart and mind to God. Put yourself in His presence.
Pray your Morning Offering and the following prayer:

Dear Lord Jesus, thank you for the gift of this time of
preparation to make my consecration to You. Please open
my heart fully to Your graces. Dear Mother Mary, you
were ready to ascend the thirteen steps to the temple
when you were presented at the tender age of three.
Though so young, because of God's amazing mystery
and grace, you were ready to do God's work. Take me as
your own child, and please grant me the graces I need to
ascend toward the Almighty. Dear Saint Joseph, be my
steady guide today. Amen.

Teaching for Parents

We focus today on the elements in a perfect Marian consecration.

The Nature of Perfect Devotion to the Blessed Virgin
or Perfect Consecration to Jesus Christ

As all perfection consists in our being conformed, united,
and consecrated to Jesus, it naturally follows that the most
perfect of all devotions is that which conforms, unites, and
consecrates us most completely to Jesus. Now, of all God's
creatures Mary is the most conformed to Jesus. It therefore
follows that, of all devotions, devotion to her makes for the
most effective consecration and conformity to him. The
more one is consecrated to Mary, the more one is consecrated to Jesus.

That is why perfect consecration to Jesus is but a perfect and complete consecration of oneself to the Blessed Virgin, which is the devotion I teach; or, in other words, it is the perfect renewal of the vows and promises of holy baptism.

This devotion consists in giving oneself entirely to Mary in order to belong entirely to Jesus through her. It requires us to give:

1. Our body with its senses and members
2. Our soul with its faculties
3. Our present material possessions and all we shall acquire in the future
4. Our interior and spiritual possessions, that is, our merits, virtues, and good actions of the past, the present, and the future

In other words, we give her all that we possess both in our natural life and in our spiritual life as well as everything we shall acquire in the future in the order of nature, of grace, and of glory in Heaven. This we do without any reservation, not even of a penny, a hair, or the smallest good deed. And we give for all eternity without claiming or expecting, in return for our offering and our service, any other reward than the honor of belonging to Our Lord through Mary and in Mary, even though our Mother were not—as, in fact, she always is—the most generous and appreciative of all God's creatures.[54]

Teaching for Children

Saint Louis teaches us that when we consecrate ourselves to Jesus through Mary, it is "the perfect renewal of the vows and promises of holy baptism." Talk to the children about their baptisms. Let them

---

[54] Saint Louis Marie de Montfort, *True Devotion*, nos. 120–121.

know that the powerful sacrament not only purified them and made them new but also brought them into the Body of Christ. They became members of the Church as the holy waters of baptism flowed over their little heads. When they consecrate their lives to Jesus through Mary, they will renew their vows and promises on their own and not through their godparents, as on their baptismal days.

In our teaching today, Saint Louis emphasizes that we need to give ourselves entirely to Mother Mary and trust her with our lives. We give her everything, knowing that she is a loving Mother who wants what is best for our souls and trusting wholeheartedly in her care for us. Give a couple of examples to your children about how they can trust Mary with their every need and really with their whole lives. If possible, use an example from your own life.

Carry Out

Do your best to learn more about Mary and strive to imitate her. After all, she was Jesus' first disciple! As well, she always leads us to her Son! We need to get to know her better. We do this through prayer and through learning more about her. Many of the saints and popes have had a strong devotion to the Blessed Virgin. Today or sometime soon, endeavor to get to know Mary more. The more you get to know her and talk to her, the more you will love her.

Family Prayer

Saint Louis prescribes four prayers for today and throughout this phase of preparation. They are the Litany of the Holy Spirit, the Litany of the Blessed Virgin, the Ave Maris Stella, and Saint Louis de Montfort's Prayer to Mary. You can find them in the appendix "Prayers for Consecration Preparation."

Find time today to pray the holy Rosary.

Evening

Saint Maximilian Kolbe (1894–1941) said, "When we dedicate ourselves to Mary, we become instruments in her hands, just as she is an instrument in God's hands. Let us then be guided by her, for she will provide for the needs of body and soul and overcome all difficulties and anxieties." That said, do your best to trust Mary with all of your anxieties, difficulties, and concerns. Give them right over to her loving and capable hands. Rest well tonight knowing that the Mother of God loves you and is accompanying you and your family on your journey of preparation for your family consecration.

Mary, My Mother

Dearest Mother Mary, thank you for being with me, guiding me throughout the details of my day. Please give me strength when I grow weary of life's challenges. Help me to be a joyful help to others I meet along the way, especially the members of my own family. Thank you for being my Mother! *Hail Mary* . . .

Day 24

Let True Devotion to Mary Unite You with Jesus

Until today, Mary has not been known
sufficiently, and that is one of the reasons why
Jesus Christ is not known as he should be.[55]

—Saint Louis de Montfort

---

[55] *True Devotion*, no. 13.

Family Consecration to Jesus through Mary

Morning

Raise your heart and mind to God. Put yourself in His presence. Pray your Morning Offering and the following prayer:

Dear Lord Jesus, thank You for allowing my family to prepare our hearts to make our consecration to You. Please grant me the graces to work hard to make Your dear Mother Mary more known. Dear Mother Mary, I ask your help and entrust this new day of preparation to you. Dear Saint Joseph, help me to stay the course! Amen.

Teaching for Parents

Saint Louis teaches us about the many fundamental aspects of a true devotion to Mary, which ultimately unites us to Jesus.

Devotion to Mary Leads to Union with Our Lord

This devotion is a smooth, short, perfect, and sure way of attaining union with our Lord, in which Christian perfection consists.

This devotion is a smooth way. It is the path which Jesus Christ opened up in coming to us and in which there is no obstruction to prevent us reaching Him. It is quite true that we can attain to divine union by other roads, but these involve many more crosses and exceptional setbacks and many difficulties that we cannot easily overcome. We would have to pass through spiritual darkness, engage in struggles for which we are not prepared, endure bitter agonies, scale precipitous mountains, tread upon painful thorns, and cross frightful deserts. But when we take the path of Mary, we walk smoothly and calmly....

This devotion is a short way to discover Jesus, either because it is a road we do not wander from, or because, as we have just said, we walk along this road with greater ease and joy, and consequently with greater speed. We advance more in a brief period of submission to Mary and dependence on her than in whole years of self-will and self-reliance....

This devotion is a perfect way to reach our Lord and be united to Him, for Mary is the most perfect and the most holy of all creatures, and Jesus, who came to us in a perfect manner, chose no other road for His great and wonderful journey. The Most High, the Incomprehensible One, the Inaccessible One, He who is, deigned to come down to us poor earthly creatures who are nothing at all. How was this done?

The Most High God came down to us in a perfect way through the humble Virgin Mary, without losing anything of His divinity or holiness. It is likewise through Mary that we poor creatures must ascend to almighty God in a perfect manner without having anything to fear....

This devotion to our Lady is a sure way to go to Jesus and to acquire holiness through union with Him. The devotion which I teach is not new. Its history goes back so far that the time of its origin cannot be ascertained with any precision, as Fr. Boudon, who died a holy death a short time ago, states in a book which he wrote on this devotion. It is however certain that for more than seven hundred years we find traces of it in the Church....

This devotion is a safe means of going to Jesus Christ, because it is Mary's role to lead us safely to her Son; just as it is the role of our Lord to lead us to the eternal Father.[56]

Teaching for Children

Saint Louis taught succinctly that true devotion to the Blessed Virgin Mary "is a smooth, short, perfect, and sure way of attaining union with Our Lord, in which Christian perfection consists." He then elaborates upon these points.

Talk to your children about what it means to attain union with Our Lord. What exactly does this mean? The *Catechism of the Catholic Church* states, "Spiritual progress tends toward ever more intimate union with Christ. This union is called 'mystical' because it participates in the mystery of Christ through the sacraments — 'the holy mysteries' — and, in him, in the mystery of the Holy Trinity. God calls us all to this intimate union with him, even if the special graces or extraordinary signs of this mystical life are granted only to some for the sake of manifesting the gratuitous gift given to all" (no. 2014).

Why should we desire to be united to God? First of all, because God calls us to it. Secondly, it only makes sense that being united to God helps us to become holy and to be able to enter Heaven at the proper time. As Catholics, we should always strive for holiness and union with God. We need to turn away from the tempting false promises of our culture that attempt to seduce us into following false gods. These include success according to the world's standards, seeking pleasures of all kinds, disregard for God's most vulnerable, and so on. The evil one masks his road to Hell with illusions of

[56] Saint Louis Marie de Montfort, *True Devotion*, nos. 213–225.

happiness in this world. We know as Christians that Jesus instructed us to deny ourselves, pick up our crosses, and follow Him. *He* leads us to Heaven! Not the evil one! Talk to your children about these truths in a way that they will understand.

Finish your teaching by emphasizing that a true devotion to Mother Mary will help keep our eyes on Heaven and its rewards. Mary will prevent us from sinking! We need to turn to her of-ten—many times a day.

Carry Out

When gathered at the table, remind your family what Saint Louis said in the verse above: "Mary has not been known sufficiently, and that is one of the reasons why Jesus Christ is not known as he should be." Ask everyone if they would like to help make Jesus and Mary more known. Hopefully, everyone will answer with an exuberant yes! Put your heads together and jot down some ideas about how you can all accomplish this. In addition to your ideas, which will hopefully be put into practice, remember that your preparation for your family consecration will accomplish this as well. So dig into it heartily!

Family Prayer

Saint Louis prescribes four prayers for today and throughout this phase of preparation. They are the Litany of the Holy Spirit, the Litany of the Blessed Virgin, the Ave Maris Stella, and Saint Louis de Montfort's Prayer to Mary. You can find them in the appendix "Prayers for Consecration Preparation."

Find time today to pray the holy Rosary.

Family Consecration to Jesus through Mary

Evening

Evening is here, and it's that time to ponder your day. This practice will help you to continue your preparation and make improvements along the way. Help and encourage your family members to pause to consider their words and actions today and to ask forgiveness for any shortcomings. Help your children with this. Always praise them for their great efforts!

Continue to strive for holiness and unplug every day from unnecessary technology during this time of preparation as you work hard on your preparation to make your consecration.

Bless your family with holy water before going to bed. Send everyone to bed with hugs and kisses, emphasizing that they are loved! Remind them to pray to their guardian angels.

Mary, My Mother

Dearest Mary, my Mother, please keep me close to your Immaculate Heart so that I will be safe from the devil's tactics. Please grant me all the graces I need to come closer to you and your Son, Jesus. Please help me to be courageous in making you and Jesus more known. *Hail Mary . . .*

Day 25

Receive the Gifts of True Devotion

A few times She [Saint Elizabeth] merited to
see most holy Mary during her prayers, ravished
and raised from the ground and altogether
filled with divine splendor and beauty, so that
she could not have looked upon her face, nor
remain alive in her presence, if she had not
been strengthened by divine power.[57]

—Venerable Mary of Agreda

[57] *Mystical City of God*, vol. 2, no. 239.

Family Consecration to Jesus through Mary

Morning

Raise your heart and mind to God. Put yourself in His presence.
Pray your Morning Offering and the following prayer:

Dear Lord Jesus, thank You for the gift of my family and
a new day to work hard on my pilgrimage of holiness.
Shield me from life's dangers. Dear Mother Mary, you are
my Mother and my glorious and heroic example to follow.
You teach me how to be dedicated to the Lord and to be
present to those who suffer. I entrust my day to you. Dear
Saint Joseph, please pray for me. Amen.

Teaching for Parents

Saint Louis tells us today about the splendid effects (gifts) associ-
ated with a true devotion to the Blessed Virgin Mary.

Wonderful Effects of the Devotion

My dear friend, be sure that if you remain faithful to the
interior and exterior practices of this devotion which I will
point out, the following effects will be produced in your soul:

Knowledge of our unworthiness. By the light which the
Holy Spirit will give you through Mary, His faithful spouse,
you will perceive the evil inclinations of your fallen nature
and how incapable you are of any good apart from that which
God produces in you as Author of nature and of grace. As
a consequence of this knowledge, you will despise yourself
and think of yourself only as an object of repugnance....
Finally, the humble Virgin Mary will share her humility with
you so that, although you regard yourself with distaste and

desire to be disregarded by others, you will not look down slightingly upon anyone.

A *share in Mary's faith.* Mary will share her faith with you. Her faith on earth was stronger than that of all the patriarchs, prophets, apostles, and saints.... Therefore, the more you gain the friendship of this noble Queen and faithful Virgin, the more you will be inspired by faith in your daily life. It will cause you to depend less upon sensible and extraordinary feelings. For it is a lively faith animated by love enabling you to do everything from no other motive than that of pure love....

The gift of pure love. The Mother of fair love will rid your heart of all scruples and inordinate servile fear. She will open and enlarge it to obey the commandments of her Son with alacrity and with the holy freedom of the children of God. She will fill your heart with pure love of which she is the treasury. You will then cease to act as you did before, out of fear of the God who is love, but rather out of pure love....

Great confidence in God and in Mary. Our Blessed Lady will fill you with unbounded confidence in God and in herself, because you will no longer approach Jesus by yourself but always through Mary, your loving Mother....

Communication of the spirit of Mary. The soul of Mary will be communicated to you to glorify the Lord. Her spirit will take the place of yours to rejoice in God, her Savior, but only if you are faithful to the practices of this devotion....

Transformation into the likeness of Jesus. If Mary, the Tree of Life, is well cultivated in our soul by fidelity to this devotion, she will in due time bring forth her fruit, which is none other than Jesus....

Family Consecration to Jesus through Mary

The greater glory of Christ. If you live this devotion sincerely, you will give more glory to Jesus in a month than in many years of a more demanding devotion.[58]

Teaching for Children

In the back of this book is a section on interior and exterior practices recommended by Saint Louis. In today's teaching, the Marian saint underscores the importance of carrying out these practices. He promises seven effects (listed above) that will take effect in your heart and soul when doing these practices.

Today is a perfect day to look at that list of practices with your children. Choose a few to do soon. You might consider adding a couple of these practices to your daily repertoire of prayers and devotions.

Take, for instance, number 11 under "Exterior Practices," which is about images of Mary. Walk around your home with your children and count the images of Mary. Do you have any ideas about adding to what you already have? Carve out some time soon to sit at the table with your family to create images of Mary. As well, consider purchasing a special image (a print, an icon, or a statue) and have it blessed for your home.

You might talk about number 5 under "Interior Practices" (make acts of love, praise, and gratitude to Mother Mary) and discuss how to carry this out. This should become commonplace in everyone's lives. You may choose which practices to discuss, or let your children choose.

[58] Saint Louis Marie de Montfort, *True Devotion*, nos. 213–225.

Carry Out

Plan to make a family visit to Jesus in the Blessed Sacrament today or soon. In the verse that begins today, Venerable Mary of Agreda explains that when the Blessed Mother visited her cousin Saint Elizabeth, there were times when the older cousin observed her younger cousin, pregnant with Jesus, kneeling in prayer. She watched as Mary was "ravished and raised from the ground and altogether filled with divine splendor and beauty."

Can we even imagine this? I give thanks to God that this and other revelations were made known to the mystic Venerable Mary of Agreda so that we can know about them and be edified. We will experience and see truly amazing things when we get to Heaven. Right now, we have only a mere whisper of a glimpse of the glorious beauty.

Saint Elizabeth grew in great holiness when her Lord Jesus was residing in His Mother Mary's womb while she was visiting Elizabeth's humble home. "Without attracting the attention of most holy Mary, [Saint Elizabeth] prostrated herself and knelt in her presence, and adored the incarnate Word in the virginal temple of the most holy Mother," according to Venerable Mary of Agreda. Go to Jesus in the Blessed Sacrament and profoundly adore Him with all your heart. Be like Saint Elizabeth and Mother Mary. Learn and grow in holiness in Jesus' presence.

Family Prayer

Saint Louis prescribes four prayers for today and throughout this phase of preparation. They are the Litany of the Holy Spirit, the Litany of the Blessed Virgin, the Ave Maris Stella, and Saint Louis de Montfort's Prayer to Mary. You can find them in the appendix "Prayers for Consecration Preparation."

Find time today to pray the holy Rosary.

Family Consecration to Jesus through Mary

Evening

It's time to settle everyone down. Encourage your family to dwell in the comfort of silence as much as possible. Try not to get involved in noisy activities. Consider singing songs to Mary tonight instead. Perhaps you can play a calm board game or read holy stories. Bless everyone with holy water and call upon the holy angels to protect you tonight. Rest well!

Mary, My Mother

Dearest Mary, my Mother, thank you for being my Mother. Thank you especially for your fiat—your whole-hearted yes. You responded to the angel Gabriel, "Here am I, the servant of the Lord; let it be with me according to your word." Your willingness to do your part so that God's holy will could be fulfilled is extremely edifying. Please pray for me to be generous with my life—responding positively to all that He asks of me. Please grant the graces I need to follow God's holy will without hesitation. *Hail Mary . . .*

Day 26

Invite Mary to Be Queen of Your Heart

Because of her singular cooperation with the action of
the Holy Spirit, the Church loves to pray to Mary and
with Mary, the perfect "pray-er," and to "magnify" and
invoke the Lord with her. Mary in effect shows us the
"Way" who is her Son, the one and only Mediator.

—*Compendium of the Catechism of
the Catholic Church, no. 562*

Family Consecration to Jesus through Mary

Morning

Raise your heart and mind to God. Put yourself in His presence. Pray your Morning Offering and the following prayer:

Dear Lord Jesus, thank You for the gift of my family and a new day to draw closer to You. Thank You for the gift of Your Mother, Mary. Dear Mother Mary, thank you for your fiat and your wholehearted cooperation with the action of the Holy Spirit. Please teach me to pray, and please pray along with me. I entrust my day to you. Dear Saint Joseph, please guide me and pray for me. Amen.

Teaching for Parents

Today we learn more about Mary, the Queen of heaven and earth.

Queen of Our Hearts

"If you wish to understand the Mother," says a saint, "then understand the Son. She is a worthy Mother of God."... Here let every tongue be silent.

My heart has dictated with special joy all that I have written to show that Mary has been unknown up till now, and that that is one of the reasons why Jesus Christ is not known as He should be.

If then, as is certain, the knowledge and the kingdom of Jesus Christ must come into the world, it can only be as a necessary consequence of the knowledge and reign of Mary. She who first gave Him to the world will establish His kingdom in the world....

With the whole Church I acknowledge that Mary, being a mere creature fashioned by the hands of God is, compared to His infinite majesty, less than an atom, or rather is simply nothing, since He alone can say, "I am he who is." Consequently, this great Lord, who is ever independent and self-sufficient, never had and does not now have any absolute need of the Blessed Virgin for the accomplishment of His will and the manifestation of His glory. To do all things He has only to will them.

However, I declare that, considering things as they are, because God has decided to begin and accomplish His greatest works through the Blessed Virgin ever since He created her, we can safely believe that He will not change His plan in the time to come, for He is God and therefore does not change in His thoughts or His way of acting....

Mary is the Queen of heaven and earth by grace as Jesus is king by nature and by conquest. But as the kingdom of Jesus Christ exists primarily in the heart or interior of man, according to the words of the Gospel, "The kingdom of God is within you," so the kingdom of the Blessed Virgin is principally in the interior of man, that is, in his soul. It is principally in souls that she is glorified with her Son more than in any visible creature. So we may call her, as the saints do, Queen of our hearts.[59]

Teaching for Children

Saint Louis stated, "She who first gave Him to the world will establish his kingdom in the world." He also said that God could have accomplished whatever He willed on His own, but He chose

---

[59] Saint Louis Marie de Montfort, *True Devotion*, nos. 12–38.

Mary to be the Mother of Jesus. We know that the Blessed Virgin Mary is the Queen of heaven and earth. During your preparation for your family Marian consecration, invite Mary to be Queen of your hearts.

Talk to your children about God's great love for Mary, about Mary's great love for God, about and following God's holy will. Mary was united with her Son, Jesus, throughout His life on earth and also in Heaven. She fully cooperated with grace to be able to say yes to the angel Gabriel when he came to her to reveal God's plan to her. Mary cooperated with every single grace to do all that was required of her to assist her Son in the salvation of souls.

She is still very busy saving souls and has asked that we pray for sinners and the souls of the dying so that they will turn to God. Our Lady of Fatima gave clear instructions for the faithful to pray the daily Rosary for peace in the world and to do penance for the conversion of sinners. In addition, Mary requested that we make the Five First Saturdays devotion (which is explained in the appendix "Marian Devotions and Resources" in this book) in order for her Immaculate Heart to triumph. Mary promised great graces for our salvation. Talk to your children about the importance of striving to imitate humble, holy Mary and heeding her prayer requests.

Carry Out

Today is a good day to talk over ways in which you can show your love to the Blessed Mother. Ask your children to write down (with your help) five ways that they can tell Mary they love her and five ways they can show her. As well, take a look at the Five First Saturdays devotion details in the appendix. If you are not already following this request of Our Lady of Fatima, consider doing so soon.

Family Prayer

Saint Louis prescribes four prayers for today and throughout this phase of preparation. They are the Litany of the Holy Spirit, the Litany of the Blessed Virgin, the Ave Maris Stella, and Saint Louis de Montfort's Prayer to Mary. You can find them in the appendix "Prayers for Consecration Preparation."

Find time today to pray the holy Rosary.

Evening

Each evening, during prayer before bed, try to get into the habit of doing a mental examination of your day. How did you do? Good? Bad? Could you do better tomorrow? Ask forgiveness for your shortcomings and for grace to do a better job tomorrow. Your little ones will need some help with this. Pray an Act of Contrition together.

Always end on a happy note! Praise your family for sticking with their preparation. Finish the evening with inspiring words or holy stories, lots of warm hugs, good-night kisses, and blessings with holy water. Let everyone know that they are loved!

Mary, My Mother

O Immaculata, my Mother, thank you for being with me today. Please help me to cooperate more fully with the promptings of the Holy Spirit in my life. Continue to guide me in my preparation to make my consecration to your Son, Jesus, through your loving hands and Immaculate Heart. Please make holy my efforts today, as poor as they may be, and transform them into something beautiful for your dear Son. *Hail Mary . . .*

Family Activity for Part 3

You and your family have completed the week of "Knowledge of Mary." Gather your family together today or soon to ponder Mary's beautiful virtues, which Saint Louis stated are "her profound humility, her lively faith, her blind obedience, her continual mental prayer, her mortification in all things, her surpassing purity, her ardent charity, her heroic patience, her angelic sweetness, and her divine wisdom."[60]

Give examples of how the Blessed Mother carried out the virtues. For instance, you might talk to your family about her "lively faith" in her yes to God when the archangel Gabriel appeared to her at the Annunciation. Or you might mention her "blind obedience" and having to get up and move with Saint Joseph and her Son, Jesus, at various times, including when they had to flee into Egypt. Mary's "angelic sweetness" might call to mind her caring tenderly for baby Jesus. Help your family to picture the scenes in their minds.

After this exercise, ask each family member to choose one of Mary's virtues and write about it or illustrate it using markers or

---

[60] Saint Louis Marie de Montfort, *Preparation for Total Consecration*, 37.

crayons (with your help). Then, ask them to write on their papers a simple, heartfelt promise to Mary that they will strive to be more virtuous like her, perhaps by working on the virtue that they illustrated or wrote about.

Place their papers in a basket near an image of the Blessed Mother in your home. During family prayer times, ask the Blessed Virgin to help you all to become more virtuous.

Part 4

Obtaining Knowledge of Jesus Christ

The works of Jesus and Mary can also be called
wonderful flowers; but their perfume and beauty
can only be appreciated by those who study them
carefully—and who open them and drink in their
scent by diligent and sincere meditation.[61]

—Saint Louis de Montfort

During this period, Saint Louis prescribes a study of Jesus Christ.
First, we study the Man-God, "His grace and glory; then His rights
to sovereign dominion over us; since, having renounced Satan and
the world, we have taken Jesus Christ as our Lord."

Second, we study Jesus' interior life, "namely, the virtues and
the acts of His Sacred Heart; His association with Mary in the

---

[61] Saint Louis Marie de Montfort, *The Secret of the Rosary*, trans. Mary
Barbour (Bay Shore, NY: Montfort Fathers, 1954), "Twenty-First
Rose: The Fifteen Mysteries."

mysteries of the Annunciation and Incarnation; during His infancy and hidden life at the feast of Cana and on Calvary."[62]

This period's spiritual exercises: perform acts of love of God, be thankful for the blessings of Jesus, for contrition, and resolution.

---

[62] Saint Louis Marie de Montfort, *Preparation for Total Consecration*, 56.

Day 27

Learn True Devotion to Jesus

Thy incessant prayer, my daughter, should be always
to repeat: here I am, Lord, what wilt Thou do
with me? Prepared is my heart, I am ready and not
disturbed; what does Thou wish for me to do for
Thee? These sentiments should fill thy heart in their
full and true import, repeating them more by sincere
and ardent affection, than by word of mouth.[63]

—The Blessed Mother to Venerable Mary of Agreda

[63] *Mystical City of God*, vol. 1, no. 741.

Morning

Raise your heart and mind to God. Put yourself in His presence. Pray your Morning Offering and the following prayer:

Dear Lord Jesus, thank you for the gift of today, in which I will strive to get to know You better and to praise and glorify You. Teach me the way of Your Gospel. Dear Mother Mary, I want to learn to turn to you continually today and to be more faithful to my prayers. Teach me and guide me, please. I entrust my day to your motherly care. Dear Saint Joseph, I need your help. Amen.

Teaching for Parents

Saint Louis teaches us about devotion to Jesus and that a true devotion to the Blessed Virgin Mary will robustly establish our devotion to the Lord.

True Devotion to Jesus

Jesus, our Savior, true God and true man, must be the ultimate end of all our other devotions; otherwise they would be false and misleading. He is the Alpha and the Omega, the beginning and end of everything. "We labor," says Saint Paul, "only to make all men perfect in Jesus Christ." For in Him alone dwells the entire fullness of the divinity and the complete fullness of grace, virtue, and perfection. In Him alone we have been blessed with every spiritual blessing; He is the only teacher from whom we must learn; the only Lord on whom we should depend; the only Head to whom we should be united; and the only model that we should imitate. He is the only Physician that can heal us; the only Shepherd that can feed us; the only Way that can lead us; the only Truth that we can believe; the only Life that can animate us. He alone is everything to us, and He alone can satisfy all our desires. We are given no other name under heaven by which we can be saved. God has laid no other foundation for our salvation, perfection, and glory than Jesus. Every edifice which is not built on that firm rock is founded upon shifting sands and will certainly fall sooner or later. Through Him, with Him and in Him, we can do all things and render all honor and glory to the Father in the unity of the Holy Spirit; we can make ourselves perfect and be for our neighbor a fragrance of eternal life.

If, then, we are establishing sound devotion to our Blessed Lady, it is only in order to establish devotion to our Lord more perfectly, by providing a smooth but certain way of reaching Jesus Christ. If devotion to our Lady distracted us from our Lord, we would have to reject it as an illusion of the devil. But this is far from being the case. As I have already shown and will show again later on, this devotion is necessary, simply and solely because it is a way of reaching Jesus perfectly, loving Him tenderly, and serving Him faithfully.[64]

Teaching for Children

As mentioned earlier, Saint John Paul II questioned his devotion to the Mother of God. He wondered if his great love for her might take away from his love for Christ. But he learned from Saint Louis de Montfort that he had nothing to worry about.

---

[64] Saint Louis Marie de Montfort, *True Devotion*, nos. 61–62.

Family Consecration to Jesus through Mary

Saint John Paul II said, "I found the answer to my perplexities due to the fear that the devotion to Mary, if excessive, might end by compromising the supremacy of the worship owed to Christ."

He added, "Under the wise guidance of St. Louis-Marie, I understood that, if one lives the mystery of Mary in Christ, such a risk does not exist."

Saint John Paul II explained that Mary "accompanies us in our pilgrimage of faith, hope, and charity toward an ever more intense union with Christ, only Savior and Mediator of salvation."[65]

Talk to your children about how blessed we are to have our Faith—to be Catholic and believe in Jesus and Mary. Look at the last three lines of the first paragraph of Saint Louis's teaching above. Explain in a way that your children will understand how God the Father has given us His Son, Jesus, as the perfect way to salvation. Jesus perfects us. He is our firm foundation. Without Him, we are just standing on loose sand that is carried away by winds and storms. Mother Mary helps perfect our devotion to our Lord Jesus. She provides a smooth, certain way for us to reach Jesus. We should never fear to call upon Mother Mary in all of our needs. She, the Star of the Sea, will guide us safely to our heavenly home. As well, we should do our best to stay the course in this preparation for consecration.

Carry Out

In our verse that begins our reflection today, we see that Our Lady told Venerable Mary of Agreda that she should always be ready to offer service to Jesus. Specifically, Mary told her to say, "Here I am,

---

[65] Quoted in "John Paul II Fondly Recalls Louis de Montfort's Marian Doctrine," Zenit, January 13, 2004, https://zenit.org/articles/john-paul-ii-fondly-recalls-louis-de-montfort-s-marian-doctrine/.

Lord, what wilt Thou do with me? Prepared is my heart; I am ready and not disturbed; what does Thou wish for me to do for Thee?" In addition, the Blessed Virgin said, "These sentiments should fill thy heart in their full and true import, repeating them more by sincere and ardent affection, than by word of mouth."

With this in mind, endeavor to pray from your heart, repeating your willingness to serve the Lord. Tell Him that you are ready and willing. Praying thus, you help your neighbor's soul (by serving) and your own as well.

In addition, schedule a time for your family to go to Confession soon. It's good to go to Confession on the day of your Consecration or sometime within eight days prior to it.

Family Prayer

Saint Louis prescribes the following prayers for today and throughout this phase of preparation: the Litany of the Holy Spirit, the Ave Maris Stella, the Litany of the Holy Name, Saint Louis de Montfort's Prayer to Mary, and O Jesus Living in Mary. You can find them in the appendix "Prayers for Consecration Preparation."

Find time to pray the holy Rosary.

Evening

Once again, it's time to ponder the events and encounters of the day, to thank God for His presence, and to ask forgiveness for any shortcomings. Help your children with this.

Ending the day on a positive note, bless everyone with holy water, and offer happy and inspiring stories, lots of warm hugs, and good-night kisses. Let everyone know that they are loved! Let them know too, that their guardian angels are with them to protect them!

Mary, My Mother

Dearest Mary, my Mother, I am very thankful that I am getting closer to making my Consecration to your Son, Jesus, through your loving hands and Immaculate Heart. Please gather up all of my efforts of today, pour your Motherly love over them, and please present them to your dear Son. *Hail Mary . . .*

Day 28

Persevere in Prayer

God, Who made the sun, also made the moon. The
moon does not take away from the brilliance of the
sun. The moon would be only a burnt-out cinder
floating in the immensity of space, were it not for the
sun. All its light is reflected from the sun. The Blessed
Mother reflects her Divine Son; without Him, she is
nothing. With Him, she is the Mother of Men. On
dark nights we are grateful for the moon; when we see
it shining, we know there must be a sun. So in this
dark night of the world, when men turn their backs
on Him Who is the Light of the World, we look to
Mary to guide their feet while we await the sunrise.[66]

—Venerable Archbishop Fulton J. Sheen

---

[66] Fulton J. Sheen, *The World's First Love: Mary Mother of God* (San
Francisco: Ignatius Press, 1952), 76.

Family Consecration to Jesus through Mary

Morning

Raise your heart and mind to God. Put yourself in His presence. Pray your Morning Offering and the following prayer:

Dear Lord Jesus, thank You for the gift of today, in which I will strive to pray more, find periods of silence in which to listen to You, and praise and glorify You. Teach me Your ways. Dear Mother Mary, I want to learn to learn more about your Son, Jesus. Please teach me and guide me. Take me under your motherly care. Dear Saint Joseph, you are my steady anchor. Pray for me, please. Amen.

Teaching for Parents

Today we read about Jesus' institution of the Eucharist and His praying in the Garden.

Jesus Foretells His Death

When Jesus had finished saying all these things, he said to his disciples, "You know that after two days the Passover is coming, and the Son of Man will be handed over to be crucified." (Matt. 26:1–2)

The Institution of the Eucharist

While they were eating, Jesus took a loaf of bread, and after blessing it he broke it, gave it to the disciples, and said, "Take, eat; this is my body." Then he took a cup, and after giving thanks he gave it to them, saying, "Drink from it, all of you; for this is my blood of the covenant, which is poured out for many for the forgiveness of sins. I tell you, I will never again drink of this fruit of the vine until that day when I drink it new with you in my Father's kingdom." (Matt. 26:26–29)

Jesus Prays in Gethsemane

Then Jesus went with them to a place called Gethsemane; and he said to his disciples, "Sit here while I go over there and pray." He took with him Peter and the two sons of Zebedee, and began to be grieved and agitated. Then he said to them, "I am deeply grieved, even to death; remain here, and stay awake with me." And going a little farther, he threw himself on the ground and prayed, "My Father, if it is possible, let this cup pass from me; yet not what I want but what you want." Then he came to the disciples and found them sleeping; and he said to Peter, "So, could you not stay awake with me one hour? Stay awake and pray that you may not come into the time of trial; the spirit indeed is willing, but the flesh is weak." Again he went away for the second time and prayed, "My Father, if this cannot pass unless I drink it, your will be done." Again he came and found them sleeping, for their eyes were heavy. So leaving them again, he went away and prayed for the third time, saying the same words. Then he came to the disciples and said to them, "Are you still sleeping and taking your rest? See, the hour is at hand, and the Son of Man is betrayed into the hands of sinners. Get up, let us be going. See, my betrayer is at hand." (Matt. 26:36–46)

Teaching for Children

Saint Louis gives us three readings to ponder today. Explain these readings in a way that your children will understand, emphasizing that Jesus was obedient to His Father in Heaven, seeking to do His holy will. God gave us the great gift of the Eucharist to keep company with us. As well, Jesus asks us to keep company with Him in prayer.

In addition, let us consider something quite profound from Saint Maria Faustina Kowalska, the "Secretary of Divine Mercy" who wrote in her *Diary* about Jesus in the Garden. She learned something quite incredible about perseverance in prayer, when one is having trouble or is feeling defeated or tormented. Not only should we pray more and pray longer, but those very prayers we are having trouble praying (or might give up on) are the ones that God actually needs.

Saint Faustina wrote:

> During the Holy Hour, the Lord allowed me to taste His Passion. I shared in the bitterness of the suffering that filled His soul to overflowing. Jesus gave me to understand how a soul should be faithful to prayer despite torments, dryness, and temptations; because oftentimes the realization of God's great plans depends mainly on such prayer. If we do not persevere in such prayer, we frustrate what the Lord wanted to do through us or within us. Let every soul remember these words: "And being in anguish, He prayed longer." I always prolong such prayer as much as is in my power and in conformity with my duty.[67]

Impress upon your children that we should never give up on prayer and that we can strive to be like Jesus and Saint Faustina — we can pray longer.

---

[67] Saint Maria Faustina Kowalska, *Diary*, no. 872.

Carry Out

During prayer time today, try your best not to rush through your prayers. Try to pray longer than you had planned. As well, recall Jesus' words: "So, could you not stay awake with me one hour? Stay awake and pray that you may not come into the time of trial; the spirit indeed is willing, but the flesh is weak." Do your best to make a Holy Hour in front of the Blessed Sacrament sometime soon. Bring your family. If it's too difficult to stay an entire hour, just do the best that you can, and Jesus will be pleased.

In addition, read "Crowning of Mary" (after day 34) so that you can be prepared when it comes time to crown your Queen!

Family Prayer

Saint Louis prescribes the following prayers for today and throughout this phase of preparation: the Litany of the Holy Spirit, the Ave Maris Stella, the Litany of the Holy Name, Saint Louis de Montfort's Prayer to Mary, and O Jesus Living in Mary. You can find them in the appendix "Prayers for Consecration Preparation."

Find time to pray the holy Rosary.

Evening

It's time to settle everyone down for the night. Try not to get involved in noisy activities. Encourage your family to dwell in the comfort of quiet as much as possible. Consider singing songs to Jesus and Mary tonight instead of watching television or doing other activities. Say your night prayers as a family, and encourage everyone to pray an Act of Contrition. Bless everyone with holy water, and call upon the holy angels to protect you tonight. Sleep well!

Mary, My Mother

Dearest Mary, my Mother, thank you for being with me this day as I have tried to walk forward in faith and prepare to make my consecration soon. Please be with me as I sleep. I love you. *Hail Mary* . . .

Day 29

Know and Imitate Jesus

For the Son of Man came not to be served
but to serve, and to give his life
a ransom for many.

—Mark 10:45

Morning

Raise your heart and mind to God. Put yourself in His presence. Pray your Morning Offering and the following prayer:

Dear Lord Jesus, thank You for the gift of today—another chance to come closer to You—to praise and glorify You. Please heal those who suffer so that they might know the joy of Your love. Dear Mother Mary, teach me and guide me, please. I entrust my day to your motherly care. Dear Saint Joseph, help me to be more like Jesus. Amen.

Teaching for Parents

Thomas à Kempis teaches us about getting to know Jesus more and about imitating Him.

Imitating Christ and Despising All Vanities of Earth

"He who follows Me, walks not in darkness," says the Lord. By these words of Christ we are advised to imitate His life and habits, if we wish to be truly enlightened and free from all blindness of heart. Let our chief effort, therefore, be to study the life of Jesus Christ.

The teaching of Christ is more excellent than all the advice of the saints, and he who has His spirit will find in it a hidden manna. Now, there are many who hear the Gospel often but care little for it because they have not the spirit of Christ. Yet whoever wishes to understand fully the words of Christ must try to pattern his whole life on that of Christ.

What good does it do to speak learnedly about the Trinity if, lacking humility, you displease the Trinity? Indeed, it is not learning that makes a man holy and just, but a virtuous life makes him pleasing to God. I would rather feel contrition than know how to define it. For what would it profit us to know the whole Bible by heart and the principles of all the philosophers if we live without grace and the love of God? Vanity of vanities, and all is vanity, except to love God and serve Him alone.

This is the greatest wisdom — to seek the kingdom of Heaven through contempt of the world. It is vanity, therefore, to seek and trust in riches that perish. It is vanity also to court honor and to be puffed up with pride. It is vanity to follow the lusts of the body and to desire things for which severe punishment later must come. It is vanity to wish for long life and to care little about a well-spent life. It is vanity to be concerned with the present only and not to make provision for things to come. It is vanity to love what passes quickly and not to look ahead where eternal joy abides.[68]

Teaching for Children

Our teaching today by Thomas à Kempis, known as a superb spiritual writer and teacher, emphasizes the need to get to know Jesus better in order to imitate Him. The acclaimed writer also underscores the necessity of acquiring humility. We must be humble souls in the spiritual life. Thomas à Kempis encourages all of us to let go of any ego and strive for humility.

Talk to your children today about Jesus' humble life. He was exalted by God the Father, yet He humbled Himself to serve us — to the point of death on the Cross.

Read the following passage to them:

[68] Thomas à Kempis, *Imitation*, bk. 1, chap. 1.

Family Consecration to Jesus through Mary

Let the same mind be in you that was in Christ Jesus, who, though he was in the form of God, did not regard equality with God as something to be exploited, but emptied himself, taking the form of a slave, being born in human likeness. And being found in human form, he humbled himself and became obedient to the point of death—even death on a cross. Therefore God also highly exalted him and gave him the name that is above every name, so that at the name of Jesus every knee should bend, in heaven and on earth and under the earth, and every tongue should confess that Jesus Christ is Lord, to the glory of God the Father. (Phil. 2:5–11)

Ask your children how they can try to become more humble. Ask them to give you at least one example. Emphasize that their prayers and good actions will be very helpful in acquiring the virtue of humility. Tell them to pause and ponder often their words and actions so that they can act and speak like Jesus and not as a person who thinks too much of himself.

Carry Out

Carve out some time today to read together a few Scripture verses about Jesus and humility and take time to ponder them. Here are some suggestions: Mark 10:45; 2 Corinthians 8:9; John 13:3–7; James 4:10; Proverbs 11:2; Mark 12:38–40; Colossians 3:12. See if you can get a discussion going at the dinner table.

Family Prayer

Saint Louis prescribes the following prayers for today and throughout this phase of preparation: the Litany of the Holy Spirit, the Ave Maris Stella, the Litany of the Holy Name, Saint Louis de

Montfort's Prayer to Mary, and O Jesus Living in Mary. You can find them in the appendix "Prayers for Consecration Preparation." *Find time to pray the holy Rosary.*

Evening

This evening is yet another opportunity to turn to God and ask for forgiveness for any shortcomings today. Ask family members to remind other members (nicely!), if they have observed or experienced something that could go better next time. Encourage all to offer any necessary forgiveness or sorrow — whatever the case may be. Also, as we should each day, rejoice over the goodness of the day. Ponder the most meaningful parts.

Try your best to keep a peaceful, happy, and holy atmosphere this evening. Bless everyone with holy water, and tuck them into bed with love.

Mary, My Mother

Dearest Mary, my Mother, thank you for being with me this day. I am thankful to be on this special journey to my consecration to your Son, Jesus, through your loving hands and Immaculate Heart. Please give me strength and courage to keep moving forward in faith. Please watch over me as I sleep. *Hail Mary . . .*

Day 30

Live the Cross of Jesus

Mary will share her faith with you. Her faith on
earth was stronger than that of all the patriarchs,
prophets, apostles, and saints. Now that she is
reigning in Heaven, she no longer has this faith,
since she sees everything clearly in God by the light
of glory. However, with the consent of almighty God,
she did not lose it when entering Heaven. She has
preserved it for her faithful servants in the Church
Militant. Therefore, the more you gain the friendship
of this noble Queen and faithful Virgin, the more
you will be inspired by faith in your daily life.[69]

—Saint Louis Marie de Montfort

---

[69] *True Devotion*, no. 214.

Family Consecration to Jesus through Mary

Morning

Raise your heart and mind to God. Put yourself in His presence. Pray your Morning Offering and the following prayer:

Dear Lord Jesus, thank You for the great gift that is today. Please help me to come closer to You. Dear Mother Mary, help me to be more faithful to my prayers and my preparation for my consecration to your Son, Jesus, through you. I give my day to you. Dear Saint Joseph, please teach me and guide me. I don't want to lose sight of the narrow gate. Amen.

Teaching for Parents

Today we focus on Jesus' Passion and Death.

The Crucifixion of Jesus

Then they sat down there and kept watch over him. Over his head they put the charge against him, which read, "This is Jesus, the King of the Jews."

Then two bandits were crucified with him, one on his right and one on his left. Those who passed by derided him, shaking their heads and saying, "You who would destroy the temple and build it in three days, save yourself! If you are the Son of God, come down from the cross." In the same way the chief priests also, along with the scribes and elders, were mocking him, saying, "He saved others; he cannot save himself. He is the King of Israel; let him come down from the cross now, and we will believe in him. He trusts in God; let God deliver him now, if he wants to; for he said, 'I am God's Son.'" The bandits who were crucified with him also taunted him in the same way. (Matt. 27:36–44)

Taking Up the Cross

To many, the saying "Deny thyself, take up thy cross and follow Me," seems hard, but it will be much harder to hear that final word: "Depart from Me, ye cursed, into everlasting fire." Those who hear the word of the cross and follow it willingly now need not fear that they will hear of eternal damnation on the day of judgment. This sign of the cross will be in the heavens when the Lord comes to judge. Then all the servants of the cross, who during life made themselves one with the Crucified, will draw near with great trust to Christ, the Judge.

Why, then, do you fear to take up the cross when through it you can win a kingdom? In the cross is salvation, in the cross is life, in the cross is protection from enemies, in the cross is infusion of heavenly sweetness, in the cross is strength of mind, in the cross is joy of spirit, in the cross is highest virtue, in the cross is perfect holiness. There is no salvation of soul nor hope of everlasting life but in the cross.

Take up your cross, therefore, and follow Jesus, and you shall enter eternal life.[70]

Teaching for Children

Today, we learn about Jesus' Crucifixion, how He was taunted by onlookers and unbelievers. We are instructed to learn from the Cross of Christ. We are taught that "in the cross is perfect holiness." This is certainly not a teaching we can grasp in one sitting — or in one day, or even in one month, for that matter. Learning and living

---

[70] Thomas à Kempis, *Imitation*, bk. 2, chap. 12.

the Cross of Jesus might take a lifetime. However long it takes for us to understand and to live as a true disciple of Jesus Christ is time well spent—beneficial beyond measure.

Being a true follower of Jesus is extremely countercultural. The world does not embrace suffering, nor does it believe in the beauty of the Cross of Christ. But Christians do.

Talk to your children about Jesus' selfless love for us, poured out on the Cross so that we may enter eternal life one day. Let them know that Christians believe in eternal life and the need to model their lives after Jesus so that they may enter Heaven one day. We can work each day, praying and striving to become more virtuous. Give your children some examples of how they can choose the right way and not the way of the world.

In addition, help your children to understand Jesus' countercultural teaching "Deny thyself, take up thy cross and follow me" (Matt. 16:24). Are we to be above our Lord? No, we are not. We need to live holy lives, not worldly lives. We need to be countercultural and stand up for the truth. As well, we can offer up our pains and sufferings to Jesus in union with His sufferings on the Cross and ask Him to redeem our sufferings to help our souls and the souls of others. Thus, with wholehearted, loving prayer, our sufferings can become redemptive.

Carry Out

Do some role-playing with your family. Think of a few scenarios that help to illustrate the differences between being a disciple of Christ and not being one. Consider using examples from the lives of the saints. Saint Augustine was not always holy. You might explain that he led a sinful life for many years and that when he converted, he not only became holy and a true disciple of Jesus, but he was eventually canonized a saint and made a Doctor of the Church! Give some examples from everyday life as well. These examples might include resisting temptation from peers; setting good examples; and truly listening to others in a conversation, rather than making sure that your opinion is known. Draw from your own life.

Family Prayer

Saint Louis prescribes the following prayers for today and through-out this phase of preparation: the Litany of the Holy Spirit, the Ave Maris Stella, the Litany of the Holy Name, Saint Louis de Montfort's Prayer to Mary, and O Jesus Living in Mary. You can find them in the appendix "Prayers for Consecration Preparation."
Find time to pray the holy Rosary.

Evening

As evening falls, ask everyone to take a few moments to turn to God and ask for forgiveness for any shortcomings today and for the graces to do better tomorrow. Don't forget to rejoice over the goodness of the day. What made you smile today?

Try your best to keep a peaceful, happy, and holy atmosphere this evening. Talk about Mother Mary's love for you all. Bless everyone with holy water, pray to your guardian angels, and tuck the children into bed with love.

Mary, My Mother

O Immaculata, my Mother, thank you for helping me to-day in my preparation to make my Consecration to your Son, Jesus, through your loving hands and Immaculate Heart. I wish to do better tomorrow. Please be with me tonight. *Hail Mary . . .*

Day 31

Go to Jesus in Humility

Who could ever measure the number and
greatness of the blessings which He would shower
upon a heart prepared to receive them![71]

—The Blessed Mother to Venerable Mary of Agreda

---

[71] *Mystical City of God*, vol. 2, no. 386.

Family Consecration to Jesus through Mary

Morning

Raise your heart and mind to God. Put yourself in His presence. Pray your Morning Offering and the following prayer:

Dear Lord Jesus, thank You for another day in which I will strive to come closer to You and praise and glorify You. Please heal my brokenness. Dear Mother Mary, I want to learn more from your guidance and to be more faithful to my prayers. Teach me and guide me please. I wholeheartedly give my day to your motherly care. Dear Saint Joseph, please keep me strong. Defend me against all evil. Amen.

Teaching for Parents

We read today about Jesus' great love for us in the Blessed Sacrament and about honoring the mystery of the Incarnation and praying the Hail Mary devoutly.

The Love That God Shows You in the Blessed Sacrament

Trusting in Your goodness and great mercy, O Lord, I come as one sick to the Healer, as one hungry and thirsty to the Fountain of life, as one in need to the King of heaven, a servant to his Lord, a creature to his Creator, a soul in desolation to my gentle Comforter.

But whence is this to me, that You should come to me? Who am I that You should offer Yourself to me? How dares the sinner to appear in Your presence, and You, how do You condescend to come to the sinner? You know Your servant, and You know that he has nothing good in him that You should grant him this.

I confess, therefore, my unworthiness. I acknowledge Your goodness. I praise Your mercy and give thanks for Your immense love.[72]

Honoring the Mystery of the Incarnation

Loving slaves of Jesus in Mary should hold in high esteem devotion to Jesus, the Word of God, in the great mystery of the Incarnation, March 25, which is the mystery proper to this devotion, because it was inspired by the Holy Spirit for the following reasons:

a. That we might honor and imitate the wondrous dependence which God the Son chose to have on Mary, for the glory of His Father and for the redemption of man. This dependence is revealed especially in this mystery, where Jesus becomes a captive and slave in the womb of His Blessed Mother, depending on her for everything.

b. That we might thank God for the incomparable graces He has conferred upon Mary and especially that of choosing her to be His most worthy Mother. This choice was made in the mystery of the Incarnation. These are the two principal ends of the slavery of Jesus in Mary.

Since we live in an age of pride when a great number of haughty scholars, with proud and critical minds, find fault even with long-established and sound devotions, it is better to speak of "slavery of Jesus in Mary" and to call oneself "slave of Jesus" rather than "slave of Mary." We then avoid

---

[72] Thomas à Kempis, *Imitation*, bk. 4, chap. 2.

giving any pretext for criticism. In this way, we name this devotion after its ultimate end, which is Jesus, rather than after the way and the means to arrive there, which is Mary. However, we can very well use either term without any scruple, as I myself do.

Since the principal mystery celebrated and honored in this devotion is the mystery of the Incarnation, where we find Jesus only in Mary, having become incarnate in her womb, it is appropriate for us to say "slavery of Jesus in Mary," of Jesus dwelling enthroned in Mary, according to the beautiful prayer, recited by so many great souls, "O Jesus living in Mary."[73]

Saying the Hail Mary and the Rosary

Those who accept this devotion should have a great love for the Hail Mary, or, as it is called, the Angelic Salutation.

Few Christians, however enlightened, understand the value, merit, excellence, and necessity of the Hail Mary. Our Blessed Lady herself had to appear on several occasions to men of great holiness and insight, such as Saint Dominic, Saint John Capistran, and Blessed Alan de Rupe, to convince them of the richness of this prayer.[74]

Teaching for Children

Our teachings today speak of going to Jesus in humility — of acknowledging our unworthiness, as well as trusting in His great mercy and love for us. In addition, we learn that we should stay close to the Blessed Mother and recognize that Jesus was once in her womb and depended on His Mother for everything, as should we. When

[73] Saint Louis Marie de Montfort, *True Devotion*, nos. 243–246.
[74] Ibid., no. 249.

we pray the Hail Mary lovingly, we can strive to "understand the value, merit, excellence, and necessity" of the prayer.

Slow down and pray more fervently. Remind your children about the Annunciation and Mary's humble, wholehearted fiat. If you desire, read Luke 1:26–38 to your children and talk to them about the great gift of Jesus and Mary and how we should never fear to approach them in prayer. They want only the best for us and want us to get to heaven to live in complete happiness and peace in eternity. Ask your family to think about ways that they can show more love to Jesus and Mary.

Carry Out

Today or sometime soon, go to Jesus in the Blessed Sacrament and spend some time in quiet adoration. Think of the words from today's teaching: "I come as one sick to the Healer, as one hungry and thirsty to the Fountain of life, as one in need to the King of heaven, a servant to his Lord, a creature to his Creator, a soul in desolation to my gentle Comforter." Ask Jesus to heal you and to strengthen you for the journey ahead. Encourage your family to make time for this sort of humble prayer.

In addition, encourage your family to strive to pray their Hail Marys more fervently and lovingly today and always.

Family Prayer

Saint Louis prescribes the following prayers for today and throughout this phase of preparation: the Litany of the Holy Spirit, the Ave Maris Stella, the Litany of the Holy Name, Saint Louis de Montfort's Prayer to Mary, and O Jesus Living in Mary. You can find them in the appendix "Prayers for Consecration Preparation." *Find time to pray the holy Rosary.*

Family Consecration to Jesus through Mary

Evening

Take a few moments to ponder the events of your day. Ask forgiveness for your shortcomings and for grace to do a better job tomorrow. Pray the Act of Contrition together.

Instill a healthy dose of peace and happiness in your family's hearts at bedtime. Bless everyone with holy water before going to bed. End the evening with inspiring stories, lots of warm hugs, and good-night kisses. Let everyone know that they are loved! Call upon the saints and the holy angels to be with you and your family this evening.

Mary, My Mother

Dearest Mother Mary, thank you for being with me today. Please help me to be open and ready to receive the great "number and greatness of the blessings" that Jesus will shower upon me. Thank you for helping and guiding my family. *Hail Mary . . .*

Day 32

Love Jesus above All Things

Tell [all people], My daughter, that I am Love
and Mercy itself. When a soul approaches Me
with trust, I fill it with such an abundance
of graces that it cannot contain them within
itself, but radiates them to other souls.[75]

—Jesus to Saint Faustina

---

[75] Saint Maria Faustina Kowalska, *Diary*, no. 1074.

Family Consecration to Jesus through Mary

Teaching for Parents

Today we learn about loving Jesus above all things as well as special interior practices for one who loves Mary.

Loving Jesus above All Things

Blessed is he who appreciates what it is to love Jesus and who despises himself for the sake of Jesus. Give up all other love for His, since He wishes to be loved alone above all things.

Affection for creatures is deceitful and inconstant, but the love of Jesus is true and enduring. He who clings to a creature will fall with its frailty, but he who gives himself to Jesus will ever be strengthened.

Love Him, then; keep Him as a friend. He will not leave you as others do, or let you suffer lasting death. Sometime, whether you will or not, you will have to part with everything. Cling, therefore, to Jesus in life and death; trust yourself to the glory of Him who alone can help you when all others fail.

Your Beloved is such that He will not accept what belongs to another—He wants your heart for Himself alone, to be enthroned therein as King in His own right. If you but knew how to free yourself entirely from all creatures, Jesus would gladly dwell within you.[76]

Doing Everything through, with, in, and for Mary

In addition to them [the exterior practices], here are some very sanctifying interior practices for those souls who feel called by the Holy Spirit to a high degree of perfection. They may be expressed in four words, doing everything through Mary, with Mary, in Mary, and for Mary, in order to do it more perfectly through Jesus, with Jesus, in Jesus, and for Jesus.

Through Mary: We must do everything through Mary, that is, we must obey her always and be led in all things by her spirit, which is the Holy Spirit of God. "Those who are led by the Spirit of God are children of God," says Saint Paul (Rom. 8:14). Those who are led by the spirit of Mary are children of Mary, and, consequently children of God, as we have already shown.

Among the many servants of Mary only those who are truly and faithfully devoted to her are led by her spirit.

I have said that the spirit of Mary is the spirit of God because she was never led by her own spirit, but always by the spirit of God, who made Himself master of her to such an extent that He became her very spirit....

With Mary: We must do everything with Mary, that is to say, in all our actions we must look upon Mary, although a

---

[76] Thomas à Kempis, *Imitation*, bk. 2, chap. 7.

simple human being, as the perfect model of every virtue and perfection, fashioned by the Holy Spirit for us to imitate, as far as our limited capacity allows. In every action, then, we should consider how Mary performed it or how she would perform it if she were in our place. For this reason, we must examine and meditate on the great virtues she practiced during her life, especially:

1. Her lively faith, by which she believed the angel's word without the least hesitation, and believed faithfully and constantly, even to the foot of the Cross on Calvary.

2. Her deep humility, which made her prefer seclusion, maintain silence, submit to every eventuality, and put herself in the last place.[77]

Teaching for Children

The teachings today are rich with spiritual direction. We are encouraged to realize the blessing of loving Jesus and that we should love Him above all creatures and things. When we empty ourselves of all that will take us away from God and open our hearts more fully to Him, Jesus will dwell within us. Jesus is our true Friend! Talk to the children about this. We must cling to Jesus in life and in death. He is our steady anchor and perfect compass. Others will fail us, but Jesus always leads us to Himself and our heavenly reward.

In addition, we are instructed that we must do everything through, with, in, and for Mary. Mary is our Star of the Sea. She leads us safely through every storm, escorting us to the safe harbor of her Son, Jesus. We can ask the Blessed Virgin to help us to emulate her virtues of deep Faith and humility. When we conform ourselves

---

[77] Saint Louis Marie de Montfort, *True Devotion*, nos. 257–260.

to Mother Mary, she will surely mold us into "something beautiful for God," as Mother Teresa would say.

Impress upon your family that they should deeply ponder their affections. Are they making gods out of their interests or material things and neglecting to love God to the extent that they are called as Catholics? Ask your family to think of three solid ways in which they can be sure to give their love to God and resist the temptation to get busy with too many other things.

Carry Out

Strive to do "everything through Mary, with Mary, in Mary, and for Mary, in order to do it more perfectly through Jesus, with Jesus, in Jesus, and for Jesus." Encourage your children to ask themselves, even several times a day, "What would Mary do?" in all the challenges they face, in the choices they make, and in every situation in which they are immersed. On top of that, encourage your children to ask Mary for her help. Do this yourself as well!

Family Prayer

Saint Louis prescribes the following prayers for today and throughout this phase of preparation: the Litany of the Holy Spirit, the Ave Maris Stella, the Litany of the Holy Name, Saint Louis de Montfort's Prayer to Mary, and O Jesus Living in Mary. You can find them in the appendix "Prayers for Consecration Preparation." *Find time to pray the holy Rosary.*

Evening

Settle your family. Take a few moments to quiet your mind before bed to ponder the day and to ask forgiveness for any mistakes. Help your little ones with this, praising their great efforts and pointing out areas in which better efforts are in order for the future.

End the evening with affirmation and praise, lots of hugs and good-night kisses. Let everyone know that they are loved! As well, before they go to sleep, bless them with holy water and remind everyone to tell Jesus, Mary, and the saints that they love them!

Mary, My Mother

Dearest Mary, my Mother, thank you for being with me today and every day. Please grant my family every grace that we need to make our consecration to your Son, Jesus. Knowing that you are the very best one to help me with my consecration, I place every need in your loving hands. *Hail Mary . . .*

Day 33

Do Everything in and for Mary

To contemplate Christ involves being able to
recognize him wherever he manifests himself, in his
many forms of presence, but above all in the living
sacrament of his body and his blood. *The Church
draws her life from Christ in the Eucharist*; by him she
is fed and by him she is enlightened. The Eucharist
is both a mystery of faith and a "mystery of light."
Whenever the Church celebrates the Eucharist, the
faithful can in some way relive the experience of the
two disciples on the road to Emmaus: "their eyes were
opened and they recognized him" (Luke 24:31).[78]

—Saint John Paul II

---

[78] Encyclical letter *Ecclesia de Eucharistia* (April 17, 2003), no. 6.

Family Consecration to Jesus through Mary

Morning

Raise your heart and mind to God. Put yourself in His presence. Pray your Morning Offering and the following prayer:

Dear Lord Jesus, thank You for today and my entire journey of preparation to make my Marian consecration. Please bless me with every grace that I need. Holy Spirit, please enlighten me. Dear Mother Mary, I entrust myself to your loving motherly care. Dear Saint Joseph, please help me to reach the finish line. Amen.

Teaching for Parents

We read today the necessity of the Eucharist and more about how to do everything in and for Mary, as well as how we should defend Mary's honor.

The Necessity of Communion

O most sweet Lord Jesus, how great is the happiness of the devout soul that feasts upon You at Your banquet, where there is set before her to be eaten no other food but Yourself alone, her only Lover, most desired of all that her heart can desire!

To me it would be happiness, indeed, to shed tears in Your presence from the innermost depths of love, and like the pious Magdalen to wash Your feet with them. But where now is this devotion, this copious shedding of holy tears? Certainly in Your sight, before Your holy angels, my whole heart ought to be inflamed and weep for joy. For, hidden though You are beneath another form, I have You truly present in the Sacrament.

My eyes could not bear to behold You in Your own divine brightness, nor could the whole world stand in the splendor of the glory of Your majesty. In veiling Yourself in the Sacrament, therefore, You have regard for my weakness.[79]

Doing Everything in and for Mary

In Mary: We must do everything in Mary. To understand, this we must realize that the Blessed Virgin is the true earthly paradise of the new Adam and that the ancient paradise was only a symbol of her. There are in this earthly paradise untold riches, beauties, rarities, and delights, which the new Adam, Jesus Christ, has left there. It is in this paradise that He "took His delights" for nine months, worked His wonders, and displayed His riches with the magnificence of God Himself....

In this divine place there are trees planted by the hand of God and watered by His divine unction which have borne and continue to bear fruit that is pleasing to Him.... Only the Holy Spirit can teach us the truths that these material objects symbolize....

The Holy Spirit, speaking through the Fathers of the Church, also calls our Lady the Eastern Gate, through which the High Priest, Jesus Christ, enters and goes out into the world. Through this gate He entered the world the first time, and through this same gate He will come the second time.

For Mary: Finally, we must do everything for Mary. Since we have given ourselves completely to her service, it is only right that we should do everything for her as if we were her personal servants and slaves. This does not mean that we take her for the ultimate end of our service, for Jesus alone

---

[79] Thomas à Kempis, *Imitation*, bk. 4, chap. 11.

is our ultimate end. But we take Mary for our proximate end, our mysterious intermediary and the easiest way of reaching Him....

We must defend her privileges when they are questioned and uphold her good name when it is under attack.... We must speak up and denounce those who distort devotion to her by outraging her Son, and at the same time we must apply ourselves to spreading this true devotion. As a reward for these little services, we should expect nothing in return save the honor of belonging to such a lovable Queen and the joy of being united through her to Jesus, her Son, by a bond that is indissoluble in time and in eternity.[80]

Teaching for Children

Today we learn from Thomas à Kempis about the necessity of Holy Communion. As well, Saint Louis de Montfort underscores the necessity in doing everything *in* and *for* Mary. He also speaks of "the honor of belonging to such a lovable Queen and the joy of being united through her to Jesus, her Son, by a bond that is indissoluble in time and in eternity." Who wouldn't want to be joyfully united to Jesus through Mary in a bond that is "indissoluble in time and eternity"? Count me in as one who desires this for my own soul! I wholeheartedly encourage you, dear reader, to follow the instructions and encouragement in the teachings in this book in order to achieve that mysterious and miraculous indissoluble holy bond.

Talk to your children about the absolute necessity of receiving Jesus in the Holy Eucharist, in visiting Him in adoration of the Blessed Sacrament, and in recognizing Jesus in the Eucharist as Saint John Paul II describes, "in mystery of faith and a 'mystery of

[80] Saint Louis Marie de Montfort, *True Devotion*, nos. 261–265.

light.'" We can all relive the experiences of the disciples on the Road to Emmaus! We can preach the love of Jesus to others in our own unique ways. Encourage the children to "be not afraid" to live and breathe their Faith and to do everything in Mary and for Mary so that we can allow the Blessed Virgin to unite us with her Son.

Carry Out

Endeavor to retreat into silence today as much as possible, praying, pondering, and getting your hearts and souls ready for your consecration. Unplug from any unnecessary technology and try to stay away from distractions during this holy time.

Also, read "How to Make Your Consecration," below.

Family Prayer

Saint Louis prescribes the following prayers for today and throughout this phase of preparation: the Litany of the Holy Spirit, the Ave Maris Stella, the Litany of the Holy Name, Saint Louis de Montfort's Prayer to Mary, and O Jesus Living in Mary. You can find them in the appendix "Prayers for Consecration Preparation."
Find time to pray the holy Rosary.

Evening

Settle into a peaceful evening, encouraging your family to make a mental note of their day and ask forgiveness for any shortcomings and express thanks for blessings. Help your little ones with this. Remind everyone that you will all be making your consecration tomorrow!

End the evening with inspiring and uplifting words or stories, lots of warm hugs, and good-night kisses. Bless everyone with holy water and let them know that they are loved! Get a good night's sleep!

> ## Mary, My Mother
>
> Dearest Mary, my Mother, thank you for being with me this day, helping me to walk forward in faith to make my consecration to your Son, Jesus, through your loving hands and Immaculate Heart. Please grant me every grace I need to make my consecration in the holiest, most reverent manner. I want you to be the Queen of my heart! Amen. Hail, Holy Queen ...

How to Make Your Consecration

Choose from among the consecration prayers from the next chapter, and make copies of the prayers for your family. You need not all pray the same prayer. Take them to church with you or pray them and sign them at home (wherever you will make your consecration). Saint Louis de Montfort recommends that, on the day of your consecration, you either "fast, give alms, or offer a votive candle for the good of another (or all of the above)." He recommends that you approach your consecration in a spirit of mortification by doing some kind of spiritual penance.

In addition, it is beneficial, according to the esteemed saint, to go to Confession at the time of your consecration (or during the prior eight days). If it's possible, do your Consecration in church after Mass. When receiving Holy Communion, Saint Louis suggests, give yourself to Jesus, "as a slave of love, by the hands of Mary."

Pray the words of consecration after the Mass and sign your copy of the Act of Consecration.

Day 34

Day of Family Consecration

Trusting in Your goodness and great mercy, O
Lord, I come as one sick to the Healer, as one
hungry and thirsty to the Fountain of life, as
one in need to the King of heaven, a servant
to his Lord, a creature to his Creator, a soul
in desolation to my gentle Comforter.[81]

—Thomas à Kempis

Today is a pivotal day in your life. Make it holy. Put your whole
heart into it.

Choose one or more of the following prayers or choose a Consecration prayer from appendix C. After making your family Marian
consecration and signing your pages, fold your signed copies and
put them in this book to refer to at a later time.

---

[81] *Imitation*, bk. 4, chap. 2.

Family Consecration to Jesus through Mary

Consecration Prayer for Adults
(from Saint Louis Marie de Montfort)

O Eternal and incarnate Wisdom! O sweetest and most adorable Jesus! True God and true man, only Son of the Eternal Father, and of Mary, always virgin! I adore Thee profoundly in the bosom and splendors of Thy Father during eternity; and I adore Thee also in the virginal bosom of Mary, Thy most worthy Mother, in the time of Thine Incarnation.

I give Thee thanks for that Thou hast annihilated Thyself, taking the form of a slave in order to rescue me from the cruel slavery of the devil. I praise and glorify Thee for that Thou hast been pleased to submit Thyself to Mary, Thy holy Mother, in all things, in order to make me Thy faithful slave through her. But, alas! Ungrateful and faithless as I have been, I have not kept the promises which I made so solemnly to Thee in my Baptism; I have not fulfilled my obligations; I do not deserve to be called Thy child, nor yet Thy slave; and as there is nothing in me which does not merit Thine anger and Thy repulse, I dare not come by myself before Thy most holy and august Majesty. It is on this account that I have recourse to the intercession of Thy most holy Mother, whom Thou hast given me for a mediatrix with Thee. It is through her that I hope to obtain of Thee contrition, the pardon of my sins, and the acquisition and preservation of wisdom.

Hail, then, O immaculate Mary, living tabernacle of the Divinity, where the Eternal Wisdom willed to be hidden and to be adored by angels and by men! Hail, O Queen of Heaven and earth, to whose empire everything is subject which is under God. Hail, O sure refuge of sinners, whose mercy fails no one. Hear the desires which I have of the Divine Wisdom; and for that end receive the vows and offerings which in my lowliness I present to thee.

I, _____, a faithless sinner, renew and ratify today in thy hands the vows of my baptism; I renounce forever Satan, his pomps and works; and I give myself entirely to Jesus Christ, the Incarnate Wisdom, to carry my cross after Him all the days of my life, and to be more faithful to Him than I have ever been before. In the presence of all the heavenly court I choose thee this day for my Mother and Mistress. I deliver and consecrate to thee, as thy slave, my body and soul, my goods, both interior and exterior, and even the value of all my good actions, past, present and future; leaving to thee the entire and full right of disposing of me, and all that belongs to me, without exception, according to thy good pleasure, for the greater glory of God in time and in eternity.

Receive, O benignant Virgin, this little offering of my slavery, in honor of, and in union with, that subjection which the Eternal Wisdom deigned to have to thy maternity; in homage to the power which both of you have over this poor sinner, and in thanksgiving for the privileges with which the Holy Trinity has favored thee. I declare that I wish henceforth, as thy true slave, to seek thy honor and to obey thee in all things.

O admirable Mother, present me to thy dear Son as His eternal slave, so that as He has redeemed me by thee, by thee He may receive me! O Mother of mercy, grant me the grace to obtain the true Wisdom of God; and for that end receive me among those whom thou lovest and

teachest, whom thou leadest, nourishes, and protectest as
thy children and thy slaves.

O faithful Virgin, make me in all things so perfect a
disciple, imitator, and slave of the Incarnate Wisdom, Jesus
Christ, thy Son, that I may attain, by thine intercession and
by thine example, to the fullness of His age on earth and of
His glory in Heaven. Amen.

_____

(Sign your name above.)

Date: _____

Consecration Prayer for Children
(adapted from Saint Louis Marie de Montfort)
(ages seven to eighteen)

O sweetest and most adorable Jesus! True God and true man, only Son of the Eternal Father and of Mary, Your most worthy Mother, always virgin! I adore You profoundly. I give You thanks for loving me and suffering and dying for me so that I may enter Heaven one day to be eternally happy with You forever.

I am sorry for not fulfilling the obligations of my baptismal promises. I come before You with the recourse of intercession of Your most holy Mother, whom You have given me for a mediatrix with You. Through her, I hope to obtain from You contrition and the pardon of my sins.

O immaculate Virgin Mary, you were a living tabernacle of the Divinity, where Jesus willed to be hidden and to be adored by angels and by men! Hail, O Queen of Heaven and earth, to whose empire everything is subject that is under God. Hail, O sure refuge of sinners, whose mercy fails no one. Hear the desires that I have of Jesus, the Divine Wisdom. Please receive the vows and offerings that I humbly present to you today.

I, _____, renew and ratify today in your hands the vows of my Baptism; I renounce forever Satan, his pomps and works; and I give myself entirely to Jesus Christ, the Incarnate Wisdom, to carry my cross after Him all the days of my life, and to be more faithful to Him than I have ever been before. In the presence of all the heavenly court, I choose you this day for my Mother and Mistress. I deliver and consecrate to you all that I have—my body and soul, my goods, both interior and exterior, and even the value of all my good actions, past, present, and future; leaving to you the entire and full right of disposing of me, and all that belongs to me, without exception, according to your good pleasure, for the greater glory of God in time and in eternity.

Receive, O Blessed Virgin Mary, this little offering of my slavery, in honor of, and in union with, that subjection that Jesus deigned to have to your maternity; in homage to the power that both of you have over me and in thanksgiving for the privileges with which the Holy Trinity has favored you.

I declare that I wish, as your true slave, to seek your honor and to obey you in all things. O admirable Mother, present me to your dear Son as His eternal slave, so that, as He has redeemed me by you, by you He may receive me! O Mother of mercy, grant me the grace to obtain the true Wisdom of God; and for that end, receive me among those whom you love and teach, whom you lead, nourish, and protect as your children and your slaves.

O faithful Virgin, make me in all things so perfect a disciple, imitator, and slave of the Incarnate Wisdom, Jesus Christ, your Son, that I may attain, by your intercession and by your example, to the fullness of His age on earth and of His glory in Heaven. Amen.

_____

(Sign your name above.)

Date: _____

Consecration Prayer for Adults and Children

(adults and children ages seven to eighteen)

O Mary, Virgin most powerful and Mother of mercy, Queen of Heaven and Refuge of sinners, I consecrate myself to your Immaculate Heart.

I consecrate to you my very being and my whole life; all that I have, all that I love, all that I am. To you I give my body, my heart, and my soul; to you I give everything. I desire that all that is in me and around me may belong to you and may share in the benefits of your motherly benediction. And that this act of consecration may be truly efficacious and lasting, I renew this day at your feet the promises of my baptism and my first Holy Communion.

I pledge myself to profess courageously and at all times the truths of my holy Faith, and to live as befits Catholics who are duly submissive to all the directions of the pope and the bishops in communion with him. I pledge myself to keep the commandments of God and His Church, in particular to keep holy the Lord's Day. I likewise pledge myself to make the consoling practices of the Christian religion, and above all, Holy Communion, an integral part of my life, insofar as I will be able so to do.

Finally, I promise you, O glorious Mother of God and loving Mother of men, to devote myself wholeheartedly to the service of your blessed veneration, in order to hasten and ensure, through the sovereignty of your Immaculate Heart, the coming of the kingdom of the Sacred Heart of your adorable Son, in my own heart and

Family Consecration to Jesus through Mary

in those of all men, in my country and in all the world, as
in Heaven, and so on earth. Amen.

_____

(Sign your name above.)

Date: _____

Crowning of Mary

Because the virgin Mary was raised to such a lofty
dignity as to be the mother of the King of kings, it
is deservedly and by every right that the Church
has honored her with the title of "Queen."[82]

—Saint Alphonsus Liguori

The day of your family consecration, if possible, is a very good day
to crown the Blessed Virgin Mary to show your love and honor
for her! In the encyclical *Ad Caeli Reginam*, Pope Pius XII stated,
"From early times Christians have believed, and not without reason,
that [Mary], of whom was born the Son of the Most High, received
privileges of grace above all other beings created by God.... And
when Christians reflected upon the intimate connection that obtains between a mother and a son, they readily acknowledged the
supreme royal dignity of the Mother of God."[83]

[82] *The Glories of Mary*, pt. 1, chap. I, no. 1.
[83] Pope Pius XII, *Ad Caeli Reginam*, no. 25.

Family Consecration to Jesus through Mary

Your consecration day should be a momentous occasion. Celebrate and thank the Blessed Virgin Mary today by crowning her! She has walked with you throughout your preparation for your consecration. She will continue to be with you. Your hymns and prayers, as well as your participation in crowning her will surely please the Queen of Heaven and earth. She is also the Queen of your heart!

Preparation

1. Choose two hymns to Mary (to sing at the beginning and at the end).
2. Choose a reader (parent, grandparent, guardian, or older child).
3. Plan your crowning ceremony, whether simple or elaborate, with or without a procession.
4. Be sure to have a statue (or image) of the Blessed Mother ready.
5. Make a simple crown of flowers (real or silk) for the Queen of Heaven.
6. Decide who will crown Mary (or have everyone take a turn).

Crowning Our Queen!

1. Gather your family around a statue of the Blessed Mother.
2. Sing your chosen Marian hymn.
3. Reader reads the following Scripture verse:

When Elizabeth heard Mary's greeting, the child leaped in her womb. And Elizabeth was filled with the Holy Spirit and exclaimed with a loud cry, "Blessed are you among women,

and blessed is the fruit of your womb. And why has this
happened to me, that the mother of my Lord comes to me?"
(Luke 1:41–43)

4. All pray together the Magnificat:

> My soul magnifies the Lord,
> and my spirit rejoices in God my Savior,
> for he has looked on his servant in her lowliness.
> For behold, henceforth all generations
> will call me blessed;
> for he who is mighty has done great things for me,
> and holy is his name:
> and his mercy is from age to age
> on those who fear him.
> He has shown strength with his arm,
> he has scattered the proud-hearted,
> he has cast down the mighty from their thrones,
> and lifted up the lowly;
> he has filled the hungry with good things,
> sent the rich away empty.
> He has helped his servant Israel,
> remembering his mercy,
> as he spoke to our fathers,
> to Abraham and to his posterity for ever.
> (Luke 1:46–55)

5. All pray together the following prayer by Saint Ephrem,
   a Doctor of the Church:

My Immaculate and thoroughly pure Virgin Mary,
Mother of God, Queen of the world, Hope of the
despairing: You are the Joy of the saints, the Peace-
maker between sinners and God, the Advocate of the

abandoned, the Haven of the shipwrecked. You are
the Consolation of the world, the Ransom of Captives,
the Comfortess of the afflicted, the Salvation of the
Universe. O great Queen, we fly to your protection.
We have no trust in anyone but You, O Most Faithful
Virgin. After God, you are our only hope. We call ourselves your servants. Do not allow Satan to drag us into
Hell. Hail! Most wonderful Mediatrix between God
and men, Mother of Our Savior, to whom be glory and
honor with the Father and Holy Spirit. Amen.

6. Now, it's time to crown the Blessed Mother statue or
   image. Do this in the way in which you have planned.

7. After Mary is crowned, all kneel (if possible) and show
   your love to Mary and invoke her protection by praying
   together the Litany of the Blessed Virgin, also called
   the Litany of Loreto (some of the invocations date back
   to the twelfth century). The leader can be a parent, a
   grandparent, a guardian, or an older child. All others
   will say the responses (in italics).

Lord, have mercy,
Christ, have mercy.
Lord, have mercy.
Christ, hear us.
Christ, graciously hear us.

God the Father of heaven, *have mercy on us.*
God the Son, Redeemer of the world, *have mercy on us.*
God the Holy Spirit, *have mercy on us.*
Holy Trinity, one God, *have mercy on us.*

Holy Mary, *pray for us.*
Holy Mother of God, *pray for us.*

Holy Virgin of virgins, *pray for us.*
Mother of Christ, *pray for us.*
Mother of the Church, *pray for us.*
Mother of divine grace, *pray for us.*
Mother most pure, *pray for us.*
Mother most chaste, *pray for us.*
Mother inviolate, *pray for us.*
Mother undefiled, *pray for us.*
Mother most amiable, *pray for us.*
Mother most admirable, *pray for us.*
Mother of good counsel, *pray for us.*
Mother of our Creator, *pray for us.*
Mother of our Savior, *pray for us.*
Virgin most prudent, *pray for us.*
Virgin most venerable, *pray for us.*
Virgin most renowned, *pray for us.*
Virgin most powerful, *pray for us.*
Virgin most merciful, *pray for us.*
Virgin most faithful, *pray for us.*
Mirror of justice, *pray for us.*
Seat of wisdom, *pray for us.*
Cause of our joy, *pray for us.*
Spiritual vessel, *pray for us.*
Vessel of honor, *pray for us.*
Singular vessel of devotion, *pray for us.*
Mystical rose, *pray for us.*
Tower of David, *pray for us.*
Tower of ivory, *pray for us.*
House of gold, *pray for us.*
Ark of the covenant, *pray for us.*
Gate of heaven, *pray for us.*
Morning star, *pray for us.*

Family Consecration to Jesus through Mary

Health of the sick, *pray for us.*
Refuge of sinners, *pray for us.*
Comforter of the afflicted, *pray for us.*
Help of Christians, *pray for us.*
Queen of angels, *pray for us.*
Queen of patriarchs, *pray for us.*
Queen of prophets, *pray for us.*
Queen of apostles, *pray for us.*
Queen of martyrs, *pray for us.*
Queen of confessors, *pray for us.*
Queen of virgins, *pray for us.*
Queen of all saints, *pray for us.*
Queen conceived without original sin, *pray for us.*
Queen assumed into Heaven, *pray for us.*
Queen of the most holy Rosary, *pray for us.*
Queen of families, *pray for us.*
Queen of peace, *pray for us.*

Lamb of God, You take away the sins of the world,
Spare us, O Lord.
Lamb of God, You take away the sins of the world,
Graciously hear us, O Lord.
Lamb of God, you take away the sins of the world,
Have mercy on us.
Pray for us, O Holy Mother of God.
That we may be made worthy of the promises of Christ.

Let us pray: Grant, we beseech you, O Lord God, that we
your servants may enjoy lasting health of mind and body,
and by the glorious intercession of the Blessed Mary, ever
Virgin, be delivered from present sorrow and enter into
the joy of eternal happiness. Through Christ our Lord.
Amen.

8. Reader: "Let Mary's soul be in us to glorify the Lord; let her spirit be in us that we may rejoice in God our Savior" (Saint Ambrose).
9. If possible, pray a family Rosary now.
10. End your crowning ceremony with another hymn to Mary, our Queen.

Living Your Marian Consecration

Modern times are dominated by Satan, and they
will be even more so in the future. The combat
against hell cannot be fought by men, even the
wisest ones. Only the Immaculata has received from
God the promise of victory over the devil. Now that
She is in heaven, the Mother of God is asking for
our collaboration. She is seeking souls that will be
totally consecrated to Her, to become instruments
in Her hands that will overcome Satan and extend
the Kingdom of God throughout the world.[84]

—Saint Maximilian Kolbe

We don't stop at our Marian consecration. We should earnestly
continue to live out our consecration for the remainder of our
lives, renewing it yearly. Certainly, we can renew our consecration

---

[84] Quoted in Rev. Fr. Jeremiah J. Smith, *Saint Maximilian Kolbe: Knight
of the Immaculata* (Rockford, IL: TAN Books, 1951), Kindle ed.

every day by sincerely praying our consecration prayer (or a shorter version) daily. Saint John Paul II renewed his Consecration daily.

You can see his prayer "Totally Yours" and other daily consecration prayers in the appendix. It includes prayers by Saint Teresa of Calcutta, Saint Louis de Montfort, Saint Maximilian Kolbe, and others.

As well, we are afforded countless opportunities to continue to prepare our hearts prayerfully for Jesus and Mary every single day. We continue to live out our consecration through the very details of our lives. We strive to become holy. Yes, we aim to become saints! With God's grace, it is indeed possible.

Mother Teresa, who was deeply devoted to the Blessed Virgin Mary, stated, "We must bring Mary more and more in our life; you are eager to love Jesus—pray 'Mary be a Mother to me'; 'Mary make my heart like yours—pure and humble,' again and again."[85]

I was blessed to know this humble, holy woman for about ten years. One time, when I was on complete bed rest because of a precarious pregnancy, the doctor didn't think my unborn baby would make it, due to serious complications and three previous miscarriages. Mother Teresa sent a poignant letter and a blessed Miraculous Medal to me. On an old typewriter, in the wee hours of the morning, the petite aged saint had typed:

> Do not be afraid. Just put yourself in the Hands of our Blessed Mother and let her take care of you. When you are afraid or sad or troubled just tell her so. She will prove Herself a Mother to you. Pray often: "Mary, Mother of Jesus, make me alright"; "Mary, Mother of Jesus, be Mother to me now." Enclosed is a Miraculous Medal. She has done wonders for

[85] Saint Teresa of Calcutta, "The 'True Devotion to the Blessed Virgin Mary,'" Mother Teresa of Calcutta Center, https://www.motherteresa.org/only-all-for-jesus-through-mary---total-consecration.html.

others and she will do so for you too. Just trust and pray. I
am praying for you and the baby.

Mother Teresa's words pierced my heart with a burning arrow of
hope. I share her words with you because we all need hope in troubled times. We all need to call upon Mama Mary. She is our way
to Jesus. What a gift she is!

That unborn baby, by the way, is now almost thirty years old!
Praise be to God! Thank you, Mother Mary! As well, I am wearing
that same Miraculous Medal that Mother Teresa sent to me. She
had given me others earlier, but this one is very special to me. It
got so worn that the top broke, so I have enclosed it in a small
pendant, along with a few relics. I wear it day and night.

Another thing that I will share with you is that, although I never
planned to do this, shortly after Mother Teresa went home to her
eternal reward, I started giving out blessed Miraculous Medals to
others — to the tune of tens of thousands over the years — many
times to complete strangers whom I met on my travels. No doubt,
our Lord inspired me to continue a tradition that Mother Teresa,
Saint Maximilian Kolbe, and other saints have carried out. I have
witnessed many beautiful and miraculous transformations through
our Blessed Mother's sacramental. I have no doubt whatsoever
that the recipients were moved by grace! The simple act of gifting
the blessed medals might have been a cause for a powerful turning
point in their lives. God only knows. We pray, and we trust. As
well, we move forward to help others.

I share this with you hopefully to inspire you to venture to do
the same. Pray about it. I didn't plan to write about this in this
book! I believe, however, that there is no time to waste — in many
ways, we are walking among the walking wounded. Our world
needs hope. Our world needs healing. Our world absolutely needs

Family Consecration to Jesus through Mary

God's Divine Mercy! Through Mother Mary, we can help to open a channel of grace for the hurting around us.

We are called by our Lord to move beyond our comfort zones to serve others! We will be living out our consecration though prayerful, loving works of mercy—offering prayers and sacramentals, such as the Miraculous Medal, or giving a copy of this book to someone, perhaps a friend, a family member, or a coworker, who could use it. With Mother Mary's help, fearlessly reach out in love to those in your family and people you meet. Our Lady will meet you in those grace-filled encounters. You can count on that!

Let us be encouraged by what Saint Louis de Montfort described as "very sanctifying interior practices for those souls who feel called by the Holy Spirit to a high degree of perfection." He summed it up in just four words. Let us remember them well. He said, "They may be expressed in four words, doing everything through Mary, with Mary, in Mary, and for Mary, in order to do it more perfectly through Jesus, with Jesus, in Jesus, and for Jesus."

Let us memorize these vital words, call them to mind often, and put them into practice: through Mary, with Mary, in Mary, and for Mary! Through Jesus, with Jesus, in Jesus, and for Jesus!

I'll leave you with a few poignant words from my dear mentor and friend Mother Teresa, who told me, "Pray to Our Lady—pray the Rosary very fervently, cling to Our Lady, She will surely lead you to Jesus to know His will for you."

Onward, Christian soldier!

Afterword

In God's amazing providence, a dear friend, Brother Maximillian Burkhart, OSB, who is a Benedictine monk, received permission to lend me a first-class relic of Saint Louis Marie de Montfort to have in my home during the writing of this book! I blessed myself with the holy relic every day and have asked the powerful saint for his holy guidance and intercession in the writing of this book. I have prayed that he will intercede for you as well!

In addition, you can be sure that our dear Mother in Heaven was right at the top of my list as one to whom I prayed and for whose assistance I asked. I desired that this book be exactly what it should be so that it will aid and strengthen hearts and souls in the spiritual battle that rages all around us. I believe that the Blessed Mother has indeed helped me in writing this book so that families will be protected after having placed themselves under her powerful protection by making their Marian consecration.

May the Blessed Virgin Mary, Star of the Sea, bring you and your loved ones ever closer to her Son, Jesus Christ!

Appendices

Appendix A

Interior and Exterior Practices

Saint Louis Marie de Montfort has said, "Devotion to Mary is the surest, shortest, and most perfect way to approach Jesus." His statement should heartily compel us to get to know the Blessed Mother, for she is our sure ticket to Jesus! The tireless saint lamented, "She is worthy of even more praise, respect, love, and service." Saint Louis pointed out in his writings that there are several interior and exterior practices of true devotion to the Blessed Virgin Mary. I will list all of them in this appendix to help you to make your preparation for consecration with extra fervor. Feel free to refer often to these pages for inspiration as to how you can deepen your devotion to the Blessed Mother.

In addition, you might feel inspired to do other practices to let the Blessed Mother know that you love her very much!

Interior Practices

1. Honor Mary as the worthy Mother of God with the worship of hyperdulia. Saint Louis used a peculiar word. What does "hyperdulia" mean? Simply, it means to esteem Mary and honor her above all of the saints, treating

her as the "masterpiece of grace, and the first after Jesus Christ, true God and true Man."

2. Meditate on the Blessed Mother's virtues, her privileges, and her actions.

3. Contemplate Mary's grandeurs.

4. Make acts of love, praise, and gratitude to Mother Mary.

5. Invoke her cordially.

6. Offer yourself to Mary and unite yourself with her.

7. Do all of your actions with the aim of pleasing Mary.

8. Begin, continue, and finish all of your actions by her, in her, with her, and for her so that you may do them by Jesus Christ, in Jesus Christ, with Jesus Christ, and for Jesus Christ.

Exterior Practices

1. Enroll yourself in Mary's confraternities, and enter her congregations.

2. Join a religious order instituted in her honor.

3. "Make her praises known and appreciated."

4. Give alms, fast, and undergo outward and inward mortifications in her honor.

5. Wear her "liveries, such as the rosary, the scapular, or the little chain." The "little chain" was a form of penance as well as a sign of devotion to Mary.

6. Pray the holy Rosary with attention, devotion, and modesty. In addition, pray:
   - Chaplet of six or seven decades in honor of the years Mary lived on earth
   - The Little Corona of the Blessed Virgin (three Our Fathers and twelve Hail Marys in honor of her crown of twelve stars, or privileges)

- The Office of Our Lady
- The Little Psalter of the Holy Virgin (composed by Saint Bonaventure): Saint Louis said it is "so tender and so devout that one cannot say it without being melted in it."
- Fourteen Our Fathers and Hail Marys in honor of Mary's fourteen joys
- Hymns, prayers, and canticles of the Church: the Salve Regina, the Alma, the Ave Regina Coelorum, or the Regina Coeli, according to the different seasons; or the Ave Maria Stella, the O glorious Domini, the Magnificat, or some other practice of devotion

7. Sing spiritual canticles in Mary's honor and teach others to do so.
8. Make genuflections or reverences while praying, "Ave Maria, Virgo fidelis" (Hail Mary, Virgin Faithful). Saint Louis says this will obtain from God the grace by her to be faithful to the graces of God during the day. In the evening, pray, "Ave Maria, Mater misericordiae" (Hail Mary, Mother of Mercy) to ask pardon for sins committed during the day.
9. Take care of Mary's confraternities, adorn her altars, and crown her images.
10. Have her images carried in procession. Carry a picture of Mary on your person, as Saint Louis said, "as a mighty arm against the evil spirit."
11. Have Mary's images or her name carved and placed in churches, or in houses, or on the gates and entrances into cities, churches, and houses.
12. Consecrate yourself to Mary in a special solemn manner (which is what you will do on your consecration day)!

Appendix B

Prayers for Consecration Preparation

Prayers for Part 1: Spirit of the World

Veni Creator Spiritus
(Come Holy Spirit, Creator Blest)

This hymn is attributed to Rabanus Maurus (776–856). It is used at Vespers, on Pentecost, for the dedication of a Church, for confirmation, and for holy orders, and whenever the Holy Spirit is solemnly invoked. A partial indulgence is granted to the faithful who recite it. A plenary indulgence is granted if it is recited on January 1 or on the feast of Pentecost.

Come, Holy Spirit, Creator blest,
And in our souls take up Thy rest;
Come with Thy grace and heavenly aid
To fill the hearts which Thou hast made.

O comforter, to Thee we cry,
O heavenly gift of God Most High,
O fount of life and fire of love,
And sweet anointing from above.

Family Consecration to Jesus through Mary

Thou in Thy sevenfold gifts are known;
Thou, finger of God's hand we own;
Thou, promise of the Father, Thou
Who dost the tongue with power imbue.

Kindle our sense from above,
And make our hearts o'erflow with love;
With patience firm and virtue high
The weakness of our flesh supply.

Far from us drive the foe we dread,
And grant us Thy peace instead;
So shall we not, with Thee for guide,
Turn from the path of life aside.

Oh, may Thy grace on us bestow
The Father and the Son to know;
And Thee, through endless times confessed,
Of both the eternal Spirit blest.

Now to the Father and the Son,
Who rose from death, be glory given,
With Thou, O Holy Comforter,
Henceforth by all in earth and heaven. Amen.

Ave Maris Stella

Hail, bright star of ocean,
God's own Mother blest,
Ever sinless Virgin,
Gate of heavenly rest.

Taking that sweet Ave
Which from Gabriel came,

Peace confirm within us,
Changing Eva's name.

Break the captives' fetters,
Light on blindness pour,
All our ills expelling,
Every bliss implore.

Show thyself a Mother;
May the Word Divine,
Born for us thy Infant,
Hear our prayers through thine.

Virgin all excelling,
Mildest of the mild,
Freed from guilt, preserve us,
Pure and undefiled.

Keep our life all spotless,
Make our way secure,
Till we find in Jesus,
Joy forevermore.

Through the highest heaven
To the Almighty Three,
Father, Son and Spirit,
One same glory be. Amen.

Magnificat

The Magnificat is the only prayer we have that was composed by the Blessed Mother. Saint Louis de Montfort said, "It is the greatest offering of praise that God ever received under the law of grace. On the one hand, it is the most humble hymn of thanksgiving and, on the other, it is the most sublime and exalted. Contained in it are mysteries so great and so hidden that even the angels do not understand them."[86] That said, this is a prayer we should pray often.

My soul proclaims the greatness of the Lord,
My spirit rejoices in God my Savior
For he has looked with favor on his lowly servant.
From this day all generations will call me blessed:
The Almighty has done great things for me,
And holy is his Name.
He has mercy on those who fear him
In every generation.
He has shown the strength of his arm,
He has scattered the proud in their conceit.
He has cast down the mighty from their thrones,
And has lifted up the lowly.
He has filled the hungry with good things,
And the rich he has sent away empty.
He has come to the help of his servant Israel
for he remembered his promise of mercy,
the promise he made to our fathers,
To Abraham and his children forever.
Glory to the Father and to the Son and to the Holy Spirit,
    as it was in the beginning, is now, and will be forever.
    Amen.

[86] Saint Louis Marie de Montfort, *True Devotion*, no. 255.

Prayers for Part 2: Knowledge of Self

Litany of the Holy Spirit

Lord, have mercy on us.

Christ, have mercy on us.

Lord, have mercy on us.

Father all powerful, *have mercy on us.*

Jesus, Eternal Son of the Father, Redeemer of the world, *save us.*

Spirit of the Father and the Son, boundless life of both, *sanctify us.*

Holy Trinity, *hear us.*

Holy Spirit, who proceedest from the Father and the Son, *enter our hearts.*

Holy Spirit, who art equal to the Father and the Son, *enter our hearts.*

Promise of God the Father, *have mercy on us.*

Ray of heavenly light, *have mercy on us.*

Author of all good, *have mercy on us.*

Source of heavenly water, *have mercy on us.*

Consuming fire, *have mercy on us.*

Ardent charity, *have mercy on us.*

Spiritual unction, *have mercy on us.*

Spirit of love and truth, *have mercy on us.*

Spirit of wisdom and understanding, *have mercy on us.*

Spirit of counsel and fortitude, *have mercy on us.*

Spirit of knowledge and piety, *have mercy on us.*

Spirit of the fear of the Lord, *have mercy on us.*

Spirit of grace and prayer, *have mercy on us.*

Spirit of peace and meekness, *have mercy on us.*

Family Consecration to Jesus through Mary

Spirit of modesty and innocence, *have mercy on us.*
Holy Spirit, the Comforter, *have mercy on us.*
Holy Spirit, the Sanctifier, *have mercy on us.*
Holy Spirit, who governest the Church, *have mercy on us.*
Gift of God, the Most High, *have mercy on us.*
Spirit who fillest the universe, *have mercy on us.*
Spirit of the adoption of the children of God,
    have mercy on us.
Holy Spirit, *inspire us with horror of sin.*
Holy Spirit, *come and renew the face of the earth.*
Holy Spirit, *shed Thy light in our souls.*
Holy Spirit, *engrave Thy law in our hearts.*
Holy Spirit, *inflame us with the flame of Thy love.*
Holy Spirit, *open to us the treasures of Thy graces.*
Holy Spirit, *teach us to pray well.*
Holy Spirit, *enlighten us with Thy heavenly inspirations.*
Holy Spirit, *lead us in the way of salvation.*
Holy Spirit, *grant us the only necessary knowledge.*
Holy Spirit, *inspire in us the practice of good.*
Holy Spirit, *grant us the merits of all virtues.*
Holy Spirit, *make us persevere in justice.*
Holy Spirit, *be Thou our everlasting reward.*

Lamb of God, who takest away the sins of the world,
    send us Thy Holy Spirit.
Lamb of God, who takest away the sins of the world,
    pour down into our souls the gifts of the Holy Spirit.
Lamb of God, who takest away the sins of the world,
    grant us the Spirit of wisdom and piety.

V. Come, Holy Spirit! Fill the hearts of Thy faithful,
R. And enkindle in them the fire of Thy love.

Let us pray: Grant, O merciful Father, that Thy Divine Spirit may enlighten, inflame, and purify us, that He may penetrate us with His heavenly dew and make us fruitful in good works, through Our Lord Jesus Christ, Thy Son, who with Thee, in the unity of the same Spirit, liveth and reigneth forever and ever. *Amen.*

Litany of the Blessed Virgin
(approved by Pope Sixtus V in 1587)

Lord, have mercy,
Christ, have mercy.
Lord, have mercy.
Christ, hear us.
Christ, graciously hear us.

God the Father of heaven, *have mercy on us.*
God the Son, Redeemer of the world, *have mercy on us.*
God the Holy Spirit, *have mercy on us.*
Holy Trinity, one God, *have mercy on us.*

Holy Mary, *pray for us.*
Holy Mother of God, *pray for us.*
Holy Virgin of virgins, *pray for us.*
Mother of Christ, *pray for us.*
Mother of the Church, *pray for us.*
Mother of divine grace, *pray for us.*
Mother most pure, *pray for us.*
Mother most chaste, *pray for us.*
Mother inviolate, *pray for us.*
Mother undefiled, *pray for us.*
Mother most amiable, *pray for us.*

Family Consecration to Jesus through Mary

Mother most admirable, *pray for us.*
Mother of good counsel, *pray for us.*
Mother of our Creator, *pray for us.*
Mother of our Savior, *pray for us.*
Virgin most prudent, *pray for us.*
Virgin most venerable, *pray for us.*
Virgin most renowned, *pray for us.*
Virgin most powerful, *pray for us.*
Virgin most merciful, *pray for us.*
Virgin most faithful, *pray for us.*
Mirror of justice, *pray for us.*
Seat of wisdom, *pray for us.*
Cause of our joy, *pray for us.*
Spiritual vessel, *pray for us.*
Vessel of honor, *pray for us.*
Singular vessel of devotion, *pray for us.*
Mystical rose, *pray for us.*
Tower of David, *pray for us.*
Tower of ivory, *pray for us.*
House of gold, *pray for us.*
Ark of the covenant, *pray for us.*
Gate of heaven, *pray for us.*
Morning star, *pray for us.*
Health of the sick, *pray for us.*
Refuge of sinners, *pray for us.*
Comforter of the afflicted, *pray for us.*
Help of Christians, *pray for us.*
Queen of angels, *pray for us.*
Queen of patriarchs, *pray for us.*
Queen of prophets, *pray for us.*
Queen of apostles, *pray for us.*
Queen of martyrs, *pray for us.*

Queen of confessors, *pray for us.*
Queen of virgins, *pray for us.*
Queen of all saints, *pray for us.*
Queen conceived without original sin, *pray for us.*
Queen assumed into Heaven, *pray for us.*
Queen of the most holy Rosary, *pray for us.*
Queen of families, *pray for us.*
Queen of peace, *pray for us.*

Lamb of God, You take away the sins of the world,
Spare us, O Lord.
Lamb of God, You take away the sins of the world,
Graciously hear us, O Lord.
Lamb of God, you take away the sins of the world,
Have mercy on us.

Pray for us, O holy Mother of God.
That we may be made worthy of the promises of Christ.

Let us pray: Grant, we beseech you, O Lord God, that we
your servants may enjoy lasting health of mind and body, and
by the glorious intercession of the Blessed Mary, ever Virgin,
be delivered from present sorrow and enter into the joy of
eternal happiness. Through Christ our Lord. *Amen.*

Ave Maris Stella

Hail, bright star of ocean,
God's own Mother blest,
Ever sinless Virgin,
Gate of heavenly rest.

Taking that sweet Ave
Which from Gabriel came,

Family Consecration to Jesus through Mary

Peace confirm within us,
Changing Eva's name.

Break the captives' fetters,
Light on blindness pour,
All our ills expelling,
Every bliss implore.

Show thyself a Mother;
May the Word Divine,
Born for us thy Infant,
Hear our prayers through thine.

Virgin all excelling,
Mildest of the mild,
Freed from guilt, preserve us,
Pure and undefiled.

Keep our life all spotless,
Make our way secure,
Till we find in Jesus,
Joy forevermore.

Through the highest heaven
To the Almighty Three,
Father, Son and Spirit,
One same glory be. Amen.

Prayers for Part 3: Knowledge of Mary

Litany of the Holy Spirit

Lord, have mercy on us.

Christ, have mercy on us.

Lord, have mercy on us.

Father all powerful, *have mercy on us.*

Jesus, Eternal Son of the Father, Redeemer of the world,
> *save us.*

Spirit of the Father and the Son, boundless life of both,
> *sanctify us.*

Holy Trinity, *hear us.*

Holy Spirit, who proceedest from the Father and the Son,
> *enter our hearts.*

Holy Spirit, who art equal to the Father and the Son, *enter
our hearts.*

Promise of God the Father, *have mercy on us.*

Ray of heavenly light, *have mercy on us.*

Author of all good, *have mercy on us.*

Source of heavenly water, *have mercy on us.*

Consuming fire, *have mercy on us.*

Ardent charity, *have mercy on us.*

Spiritual unction, *have mercy on us.*

Spirit of love and truth, *have mercy on us.*

Spirit of wisdom and understanding, *have mercy on us.*

Spirit of counsel and fortitude, *have mercy on us.*

Spirit of knowledge and piety, *have mercy on us.*

Spirit of the fear of the Lord, *have mercy on us.*

Spirit of grace and prayer, *have mercy on us.*

Spirit of peace and meekness, *have mercy on us.*

Spirit of modesty and innocence, *have mercy on us.*

Family Consecration to Jesus through Mary

Holy Spirit, the Comforter, *have mercy on us.*
Holy Spirit, the Sanctifier, *have mercy on us.*
Holy Spirit, who governest the Church, *have mercy on us.*
Gift of God, the Most High, *have mercy on us.*
Spirit who fillest the universe, *have mercy on us.*
Spirit of the adoption of the children of God,
    have mercy on us.
Holy Spirit, *inspire us with horror of sin.*
Holy Spirit, *come and renew the face of the earth.*
Holy Spirit, *shed Thy light in our souls.*
Holy Spirit, *engrave Thy law in our hearts.*
Holy Spirit, *inflame us with the flame of Thy love.*
Holy Spirit, *open to us the treasures of Thy graces.*
Holy Spirit, *teach us to pray well.*
Holy Spirit, *enlighten us with Thy heavenly inspirations.*
Holy Spirit, *lead us in the way of salvation.*
Holy Spirit, *grant us the only necessary knowledge.*
Holy Spirit, *inspire in us the practice of good.*
Holy Spirit, *grant us the merits of all virtues.*
Holy Spirit, *make us persevere in justice.*
Holy Spirit, *be Thou our everlasting reward.*

Lamb of God, who takest away the sins of the world,
    send us Thy Holy Spirit.
Lamb of God, who takest away the sins of the world,
    pour down into our souls the gifts of the Holy Spirit.
Lamb of God, who takest away the sins of the world,
    grant us the Spirit of wisdom and piety.

V. Come, Holy Spirit! Fill the hearts of Thy faithful,
R. And enkindle in them the fire of Thy love.

Prayers for Consecration Preparation

Let us pray: Grant, O merciful Father, that Thy Divine
Spirit may enlighten, inflame, and purify us, that He
may penetrate us with His heavenly dew and make us
fruitful in good works, through Our Lord Jesus Christ,
Thy Son, who with Thee, in the unity of the same
Spirit, liveth and reigneth forever and ever. *Amen.*

Litany of the Blessed Virgin

Lord, have mercy,
Christ, have mercy.
Lord, have mercy.
Christ, hear us.
Christ, graciously hear us.

God the Father of heaven, *have mercy on us.*
God the Son, Redeemer of the world, *have mercy on us.*
God the Holy Spirit, *have mercy on us.*
Holy Trinity, one God, *have mercy on us.*

Holy Mary, *pray for us.*
Holy Mother of God, *pray for us.*
Holy Virgin of virgins, *pray for us.*
Mother of Christ, *pray for us.*
Mother of the Church, *pray for us.*
Mother of divine grace, *pray for us.*
Mother most pure, *pray for us.*
Mother most chaste, *pray for us.*
Mother inviolate, *pray for us.*
Mother undefiled, *pray for us.*
Mother most amiable, *pray for us.*
Mother most admirable, *pray for us.*
Mother of good counsel, *pray for us.*

Family Consecration to Jesus through Mary

Mother of our Creator, *pray for us.*
Mother of our Savior, *pray for us.*
Virgin most prudent, *pray for us.*
Virgin most venerable, *pray for us.*
Virgin most renowned, *pray for us.*
Virgin most powerful, *pray for us.*
Virgin most merciful, *pray for us.*
Virgin most faithful, *pray for us.*
Mirror of justice, *pray for us.*
Seat of wisdom, *pray for us.*
Cause of our joy, *pray for us.*
Spiritual vessel, *pray for us.*
Vessel of honor, *pray for us.*
Singular vessel of devotion, *pray for us.*
Mystical rose, *pray for us.*
Tower of David, *pray for us.*
Tower of ivory, *pray for us.*
House of gold, *pray for us.*
Ark of the covenant, *pray for us.*
Gate of heaven, *pray for us.*
Morning star, *pray for us.*
Health of the sick, *pray for us.*
Refuge of sinners, *pray for us.*
Comforter of the afflicted, *pray for us.*
Help of Christians, *pray for us.*
Queen of angels, *pray for us.*
Queen of patriarchs, *pray for us.*
Queen of prophets, *pray for us.*
Queen of apostles, *pray for us.*
Queen of martyrs, *pray for us.*
Queen of confessors, *pray for us.*
Queen of virgins, *pray for us.*

Queen of all saints, *pray for us.*
Queen conceived without original sin, *pray for us.*
Queen assumed into Heaven, *pray for us.*
Queen of the most holy Rosary, *pray for us.*
Queen of families, *pray for us.*
Queen of peace, *pray for us.*

Lamb of God, You take away the sins of the world,
Spare us, O Lord.
Lamb of God, You take away the sins of the world,
Graciously hear us, O Lord.
Lamb of God, you take away the sins of the world,
Have mercy on us.

Pray for us, O holy Mother of God.
That we may be made worthy of the promises of Christ.

Let us pray: Grant, we beseech you, O Lord God, that we
your servants may enjoy lasting health of mind and body, and
by the glorious intercession of the Blessed Mary, ever Virgin,
be delivered from present sorrow and enter into the joy of
eternal happiness. Through Christ our Lord. *Amen.*

Ave Maris Stella

Hail, bright star of ocean,
God's own Mother blest,
Ever sinless Virgin,
Gate of heavenly rest.

Taking that sweet Ave
Which from Gabriel came,
Peace confirm within us,
Changing Eva's name.

Family Consecration to Jesus through Mary

Break the captives' fetters,
Light on blindness pour,
All our ills expelling,
Every bliss implore.

Show thyself a Mother;
May the Word Divine,
Born for us thy Infant,
Hear our prayers through thine.

Virgin all excelling,
Mildest of the mild,
Freed from guilt, preserve us,
Pure and undefiled.

Keep our life all spotless,
Make our way secure,
Till we find in Jesus,
Joy forevermore.

Through the highest heaven
To the Almighty Three,
Father, Son and Spirit,
One same glory be. Amen.

Saint Louis Marie de Montfort Prayer to Mary

Hail Mary, beloved Daughter of the Eternal Father! Hail
Mary, admirable Mother of the Son! Hail Mary, faithful
Spouse of the Holy Ghost! Hail Mary, my dear Mother,
my loving mistress, my powerful sovereign! Hail my joy,
my glory, my heart, and my soul! Thou art all mine by
mercy, and I am all thine by justice. But I am not yet suf-

ficiently thine. I now give myself wholly to thee without
keeping anything back for myself or others. If thou still
seest in me anything that does not belong to thee, I
beseech thee to take it and to make thyself the absolute
mistress of all that is mine. Destroy in me all that may
be displeasing to God, root it up, and bring it to nought;
place and cultivate in me everything that is pleasing to
thee.

May the light of thy faith dispel the darkness of my
mind; may thy profound humility take the place of my
pride; may thy sublime contemplation check the distractions of my wandering imagination; may thy continuous
sight of God fill my memory with His presence; may the
burning love of thy heart inflame the lukewarmness of
mine; may thy virtues take the place of my sins; may thy
merits be my only adornment in the sight of God and
make up for all that is wanting in me. Finally, dearly beloved Mother, grant, if it be possible, that I may have no
other spirit but thine, to know Jesus and His divine will;
that I may have no other soul but thine, to praise and
glorify the Lord; that I may have no other heart but thine,
to love God with a love as pure and ardent as thine. I do
not ask thee for visions, revelations, sensible devotion or
spiritual pleasures. It is thy privilege to see God clearly; it
is thy privilege to enjoy Heavenly bliss; it is thy privilege
to triumph gloriously in Heaven at the right hand of thy
Son and to hold absolute sway over angels, men, and demons; it is thy privilege to dispose of all the gifts of God,
just as thou willest.

Such is, O Heavenly Mary, the "best part," which
the Lord has given thee and which shall never be taken

away from thee, and this thought fills my heart with joy. As for my part here below, I wish for no other than that which was thine: to believe sincerely without spiritual pleasures; to suffer joyfully without human consolation; to die continually to myself without respite; and to work zealously and unselfishly for thee until death as the humblest of thy servants. The only grace I beg thee to obtain for me is that every day and every moment of my life I may say: "Amen, so be it, to all that thou didst do while on earth. Amen, so be it, to all that thou art now doing in Heaven. Amen, so be it, to all that thou art doing in my soul, so that thou alone mayest fully glorify Jesus in me for time and eternity." Amen.

Prayers for Part 4: Knowledge of Jesus Christ

Litany of the Holy Spirit

Lord, have mercy on us.

Christ, have mercy on us.

Lord, have mercy on us.

Father all powerful, *have mercy on us.*

Jesus, Eternal Son of the Father, Redeemer of the world,
    save us.

Spirit of the Father and the Son, boundless life of both,
    sanctify us.

Holy Trinity, *hear us.*

Holy Spirit, who proceedest from the Father and the Son,
    enter our hearts.

Holy Spirit, who art equal to the Father and the Son, *enter
    our hearts.*

Promise of God the Father, *have mercy on us.*

Ray of heavenly light, *have mercy on us.*

Author of all good, *have mercy on us.*

Source of heavenly water, *have mercy on us.*

Consuming fire, *have mercy on us.*

Ardent charity, *have mercy on us.*

Spiritual unction, *have mercy on us.*

Spirit of love and truth, *have mercy on us.*

Spirit of wisdom and understanding, *have mercy on us.*

Spirit of counsel and fortitude, *have mercy on us.*

Spirit of knowledge and piety, *have mercy on us.*

Spirit of the fear of the Lord, *have mercy on us.*

Spirit of grace and prayer, *have mercy on us.*

Spirit of peace and meekness, *have mercy on us.*

Spirit of modesty and innocence, *have mercy on us.*

Family Consecration to Jesus through Mary

Holy Spirit, the Comforter, *have mercy on us.*
Holy Spirit, the Sanctifier, *have mercy on us.*
Holy Spirit, who governest the Church, *have mercy on us.*
Gift of God, the Most High, *have mercy on us.*
Spirit who fillest the universe, *have mercy on us.*
Spirit of the adoption of the children of God,
    have mercy on us.
Holy Spirit, *inspire us with horror of sin.*
Holy Spirit, *come and renew the face of the earth.*
Holy Spirit, *shed Thy light in our souls.*
Holy Spirit, *engrave Thy law in our hearts.*
Holy Spirit, *inflame us with the flame of Thy love.*
Holy Spirit, *open to us the treasures of Thy graces.*
Holy Spirit, *teach us to pray well.*
Holy Spirit, *enlighten us with Thy heavenly inspirations.*
Holy Spirit, *lead us in the way of salvation.*
Holy Spirit, *grant us the only necessary knowledge.*
Holy Spirit, *inspire in us the practice of good.*
Holy Spirit, *grant us the merits of all virtues.*
Holy Spirit, *make us persevere in justice.*
Holy Spirit, *be Thou our everlasting reward.*

Lamb of God, who takest away the sins of the world,
    send us Thy Holy Spirit.
Lamb of God, who takest away the sins of the world,
    pour down into our souls the gifts of the Holy Spirit.
Lamb of God, who takest away the sins of the world,
    grant us the Spirit of wisdom and piety.

V. Come, Holy Spirit! Fill the hearts of Thy faithful,
R. And enkindle in them the fire of Thy love.

Let us pray: Grant, O merciful Father, that Thy Divine
Spirit may enlighten, inflame, and purify us, that He
may penetrate us with His heavenly dew and make us
fruitful in good works, through Our Lord Jesus Christ,
Thy Son, who with Thee, in the unity of the same
Spirit, liveth and reigneth forever and ever. *Amen.*

Ave Maris Stella

Hail, bright star of ocean,
God's own Mother blest,
Ever sinless Virgin,
Gate of heavenly rest.

Taking that sweet Ave
Which from Gabriel came,
Peace confirm within us,
Changing Eva's name.

Break the captives' fetters,
Light on blindness pour,
All our ills expelling,
Every bliss implore.

Show thyself a Mother;
May the Word Divine,
Born for us thy Infant,
Hear our prayers through thine.

Virgin all excelling,
Mildest of the mild,
Freed from guilt, preserve us,
Pure and undefiled.

Family Consecration to Jesus through Mary

Keep our life all spotless,
Make our way secure,
Till we find in Jesus,
Joy forevermore.

Through the highest heaven
To the Almighty Three,
Father, Son and Spirit,
One same glory be. Amen.

Litany of the Holy Name of Jesus

Lord, have mercy on us.
Christ, have mercy on us.
Lord, have mercy on us. Jesus, hear us.
Jesus, graciously hear us.
God, the Father of Heaven, *have mercy on us.*
God, the Son, Redeemer of the world, *have mercy on us.*
God, the Holy Spirit, *have mercy on us.*
Holy Trinity, One God, *have mercy on us.*

Jesus, Son of the living God, *have mercy on us.*
Jesus, splendor of the Father, *have mercy on us.*
Jesus, brightness of eternal light, *have mercy on us.*
Jesus, King of glory, *have mercy on us.*
Jesus, sun of justice, *have mercy on us.*
Jesus, Son of the Virgin Mary, *have mercy on us.*
Jesus, most amiable, *have mercy on us.*
Jesus, most admirable, *have mercy on us.*
Jesus, mighty God, *have mercy on us.*
Jesus, Father of the world to come, *have mercy on us.*
Jesus, angel of great counsel, *have mercy on us.*
Jesus, most powerful, *have mercy on us.*

Jesus, most patient, *have mercy on us.*

Jesus, most obedient, *have mercy on us.*

Jesus, meek and humble, *have mercy on us.*

Jesus, lover of chastity, *have mercy on us.*

Jesus, lover of us, *have mercy on us.*

Jesus, God of peace, *have mercy on us.*

Jesus, author of life, *have mercy on us.*

Jesus, model of virtues, *have mercy on us.*

Jesus, lover of souls, *have mercy on us.*

Jesus, our God, *have mercy on us.*

Jesus, our refuge, *have mercy on us.*

Jesus, Father of the poor, *have mercy on us.*

Jesus, treasure of the faithful, *have mercy on us.*

Jesus, Good Shepherd, *have mercy on us.*

Jesus, true light, *have mercy on us.*

Jesus, eternal wisdom, *have mercy on us.*

Jesus, infinite goodness, *have mercy on us.*

Jesus, our way and our life, *have mercy on us.*

Jesus, joy of angels, *have mercy on us.*

Jesus, king of patriarchs, *have mercy on us.*

Jesus, master of Apostles, *have mercy on us.*

Jesus, teacher of Evangelists, *have mercy on us.*

Jesus, strength of martyrs, *have mercy on us.*

Jesus, light of confessors, *have mercy on us.*

Jesus, purity of virgins, *have mercy on us.*

Jesus, crown of all saints, *have mercy on us.*

Be merciful, *spare us, O Jesus.*

Be merciful, *graciously hear us, O Jesus.*

From all evil, *Jesus, deliver us.*

From all sin, *Jesus, deliver us.*

From Thy wrath, *Jesus, deliver us.*

From the snares of the devil, *Jesus, deliver us.*

Family Consecration to Jesus through Mary

From the spirit of fornication, Jesus, *deliver us.*
From everlasting death, Jesus, *deliver us.*
From the neglect of Thine inspirations, Jesus, *deliver us.*
Through the mystery of Thy holy Incarnation, Jesus, *deliver us.*
Through Thy nativity, Jesus, *deliver us.*
Through Thine infancy, Jesus, *deliver us.*
Through Thy most divine life, Jesus, *deliver us.*
Through Thy labors, Jesus, *deliver us.*
Through Thine agony and Passion, Jesus, *deliver us.*
Through Thy cross and dereliction, Jesus, *deliver us.*
Through Thy sufferings, Jesus, *deliver us.*
Through Thy death and burial, Jesus, *deliver us.*
Through Thy Resurrection, Jesus, *deliver us.*
Through Thine Ascension, Jesus, *deliver us.*
Through Thine institution of the most Holy Eucharist,
    Jesus, *deliver us.*
Through Thy joys, Jesus, *deliver us.*
Through Thy glory, Jesus, *deliver us.*

Lamb of God, who takest away the sins of the world,
    spare us, O Jesus.
Lamb of God, who takest away the sins of the world,
    graciously hear us, O Jesus.
Lamb of God, who takest away the sins of the world,
    have mercy on us.
Jesus, hear us, Jesus, *graciously hear us.*

Let us pray: O Lord Jesus Christ, who hast said: "Ask and
    ye shall receive, seek and ye shall find, knock and it
    shall be opened unto you," grant, we beseech Thee,
    to us who ask the gift of Thy divine love, that we may
    ever love Thee with all our hearts, and in all our words

and actions, and never cease from praising Thee. Give us, O Lord, a perpetual fear and love of Thy holy Name; for Thou never failest to govern those whom Thou dost solidly establish in Thy love, who livest and reignest world without end. *Amen.*

Saint Louis Marie de Montfort Prayer to Mary

Hail Mary, beloved Daughter of the Eternal Father! Hail Mary, admirable Mother of the Son! Hail Mary, faithful Spouse of the Holy Ghost! Hail Mary, my dear Mother, my loving mistress, my powerful sovereign! Hail my joy, my glory, my heart, and my soul! Thou art all mine by mercy, and I am all thine by justice. But I am not yet sufficiently thine. I now give myself wholly to thee without keeping anything back for myself or others. If thou still seest in me anything that does not belong to thee, I beseech thee to take it and to make thyself the absolute mistress of all that is mine. Destroy in me all that may be displeasing to God, root it up, and bring it to nought; place and cultivate in me everything that is pleasing to thee.

May the light of thy faith dispel the darkness of my mind; may thy profound humility take the place of my pride; may thy sublime contemplation check the distractions of my wandering imagination; may thy continuous sight of God fill my memory with His presence; may the burning love of thy heart inflame the lukewarmness of mine; may thy virtues take the place of my sins; may thy merits be my only adornment in the sight of God and make up for all that is wanting in me. Finally, dearly beloved Mother, grant, if it be possible, that I may have no other spirit but thine, to know Jesus and His divine will; that I may have no other soul but thine, to praise and glorify the Lord; that I may have no other heart but thine, to love God with a love as pure and ardent as thine. I do not ask thee for visions, revelations, sensible devotion or spiritual pleasures. It is thy privilege to see God clearly; it is thy privilege to enjoy Heavenly bliss; it is thy privilege to triumph gloriously in Heaven at the right hand of thy Son and to hold absolute sway over angels, men, and demons; it is thy privilege to dispose of all the gifts of God, just as thou willest.

Such is, O Heavenly Mary, the "best part," which the Lord has given thee and which shall never be taken away from thee, and this thought fills my heart with joy. As for my part here below, I wish for no other than that which was thine: to believe sincerely without spiritual pleasures; to suffer joyfully without human consolation; to die continually to myself without respite; and to work zealously and unselfishly for thee until death as the humblest of thy servants. The only grace I beg thee to obtain for me is that every day and every moment of my life I may say: "Amen, so be it, to all that thou didst do while on earth. Amen, so be it, to all that thou art now doing in Heaven. Amen, so be it, to all that thou art doing in my soul, so that thou alone mayest fully glorify Jesus in me for time and eternity." Amen.

O Jesus Living in Mary

O Jesus, living in Mary,
Come and live in Thy servants,
In the spirit of Thy holiness,
In the fullness of Thy might,
In the truth of Thy virtues,
In the perfection of Thy ways,
In the communion of Thy mysteries;
Subdue every hostile power
In Thy spirit, for the glory of the Father. Amen.

Appendix C

Additional Prayers

Morning Offering

There are many variations of the Morning Offering. The important thing is to pray first thing in the morning, giving everything to Jesus in advance of your day through the Immaculate Heart of Mary and asking Him to sanctify everything for His glory.

O Jesus, through the Immaculate Heart of Mary, I offer You my prayers, works, joys, and sufferings of this day for all the intentions of Your Sacred Heart, in union with the Holy Sacrifice of the Mass throughout the world, in reparation for my sins, for the intentions of all my rela-tives and friends, and in particular for the intentions of the Holy Father. Amen.

Our Father
(The Lord's Prayer, taught by Jesus)

Our Father, who art in heaven, hallowed be Thy Name. Thy Kingdom come. Thy Will be done, on earth as it is in Heaven. Give us this day our daily bread. And forgive us our trespasses, as we forgive those who trespass against us. And lead us not into temptation, but deliver us from evil. Amen.

Hail Mary

The Hail Mary is simple prayer that most Catholics know, but when prayed earnestly, it is a powerhouse of grace! Please see Saint Louis's explanation below.

Hail Mary, full of grace, the Lord is with thee. Blessed art thou among women, and blessed is the fruit of thy womb, Jesus. Holy Mary, Mother of God, pray for us sinners, now and at the hour of our death. Amen.

Saint Louis encourages us to pray the Hail Mary fervently. He states:

When the Hail Mary is well said, that is, with attention, devotion and humility, it is, according to the saints, the enemy of Satan, putting him to flight; it is the hammer that crushes him, a source of holiness for souls, a joy to the angels and a sweet melody for the devout. It is the Canticle of the New Testament, a delight for Mary, and glory for the most Blessed Trinity. The Hail Mary is dew falling from heaven to make the soul fruitful. It is a pure kiss of love we give to Mary. It is a crimson rose, a precious pearl that we offer to her. It is a cup of ambrosia, a divine nectar that we offer her. These are comparisons made by the saints.[87]

Let us pray countless fervent Hail Marys!

[87] Saint Louis Marie de Montfort, *True Devotion*, no. 253.

Angelus

The Angelus is traditionally prayed at 6:00 a.m., noon, and 6:00 p.m., but it can be prayed anytime. The prayer dates back to the twelfth century, and in the sixteenth century, people began praying it three times a day. The Angelus reminds us of the Annunciation and calls attention to Mary's vital role in the Incarnation.

The Angel of the Lord declared to Mary:
And she conceived of the Holy Spirit.

Hail Mary, full of grace, the Lord is with thee; blessed art thou among women and blessed is the fruit of thy womb, Jesus. Holy Mary, Mother of God, pray for us sinners, now and at the hour of our death. Amen.

Behold the handmaid of the Lord:
Be it done unto me according to thy word.
Hail Mary . . .

And the Word was made flesh:
And dwelt among us.
Hail Mary . . .

Pray for us, O holy Mother of God,
That we may be made worthy of the promises of Christ.

Let us pray: Pour forth, we beseech Thee, O Lord, Thy grace into our hearts; that we, to whom the Incarnation of Christ, Thy Son, was made known by the message of an angel, may by His Passion and Cross be brought to the glory of His Resurrection, through the same Christ Our Lord. *Amen.*

Family Consecration to Jesus through Mary

Regina Caeli (Queen of Heaven)

The Regina Caeli is prayed in place of the Angelus throughout Eastertide — from Easter Day through Pentecost, the seventh Sunday after Easter. It is one of four Marian antiphons, with following versicles and prayers. It is traditionally prayed or sung after night prayer, immediately before going to sleep.

V. Queen of Heaven, rejoice, *alleluia.*

R. For He whom you did merit to bear, *alleluia.*

V. Has risen, as he said, *alleluia.*

R. Pray for us to God, *alleluia.*

V. Rejoice and be glad, O Virgin Mary, *alleluia.*

R. For the Lord has truly risen, *alleluia.*

Let us pray: O God, who gave joy to the world through the Resurrection of Thy Son, our Lord Jesus Christ, grant, we beseech Thee, that through the intercession of the Virgin Mary, His Mother, we may obtain the joys of everlasting life. Through the same Christ our Lord. *Amen.*

The Rosary

Our Lady of Fatima requested that we pray the Rosary daily for peace. She told the three shepherd children, "Continue to pray the Rosary every day." Sister Lucia, the oldest Fatima visionary, expressed, "The Most Holy Virgin in these last times in which we live has given a new efficacy to the recitation of the Rosary to such an extent that there is no problem, no matter how difficult it is, whether temporal or above all spiritual, in the personal life of each one of us, of our families ... that cannot be solved by the Rosary. There is no problem, I tell you, no matter how difficult it is, that we cannot resolve by the prayer of the Holy Rosary."

Numerous popes and saints have extolled the power of the Rosary. Saint Padre Pio, who, in his last days, insisted that the Rosary not be taken from his hands, and therefore would wash one hand at a time had said, "Our Lady has never refused me a grace through the recitation of the Rosary." Saint Louis de Montfort stated, "No prayer is more meritorious for the soul and more glorious for Jesus and Mary than a well-recited Rosary." Endeavor to pray the Rosary well and pray it daily.

There are four sets of mysteries commemorating the life of Christ that are meditated upon each day of the week, as follows:
- Sunday and Wednesday, outside of Lent and Advent: the Glorious Mysteries
- Monday and Saturday, and Sundays of Advent: the Joyful Mysteries
- Tuesday and Friday, and Sundays of Lent: the Sorrowful Mysteries
- Thursday: the Mysteries of Light

Family Consecration to Jesus through Mary

The Joyful Mysteries

First Mystery: The Annunciation of the Angel to Our Lady (Luke 1:26–38)

Second Mystery: The Visitation of Our Lady to Saint Elizabeth (Luke 1:39–56)

Third Mystery: The Birth of Jesus in Bethlehem (Luke 2:1–20)

Fourth Mystery: The Presentation of the Child Jesus in the Temple (Luke 2:22–38)

Fifth Mystery: The Finding of the Child Jesus in the Temple (Luke 2:41–50)

The Mysteries of Light
(added by Saint John Paul II in 2002 in his apostolic letter *The Rosary of the Virgin Mary*)

First Mystery: The Baptism of Jesus in the Jordan (Matt. 3:13–17)

Second Mystery: The Revelation of Jesus during the Wedding in Cana (John 2:1–11)

Third Mystery: The Proclamation of God's Kingdom and the Call to Conversion (Mark 1:14–15)

Fourth Mystery: The Transfiguration of the Lord (Luke 9:28–36)

Fifth Mystery: The Institution of Eucharist (Luke 22:14–20)

The Sorrowful Mysteries

First Mystery: The Agony of Jesus in the Garden (Matt. 26:36–46)

Second Mystery: The Scourging of Jesus (Matt. 27:24–26)

Third Mystery: The Crowning with Thorns (Matt. 27:27–31)

Fourth Mystery: Jesus' Way to Calvary and the Meeting with His Mother (Luke 23:26–32)

Fifth Mystery: The Crucifixion and Death of Jesus (John 19:17–30)

The Glorious Mysteries

First Mystery: The Resurrection of Jesus (Matt. 28:1–10)

Second Mystery: The Ascension of Jesus into Heaven (Acts 1:6–11)

Third Mystery: The Descent of the Holy Spirit on Our Lady and the Apostles (Acts 1:12–14; 2:1–4)

Fourth Mystery: The Assumption of Our Lady (Luke 1:48–49)

Fifth Mystery: The Coronation of Our Lady as Queen of the Angels and Saints (Rev. 12:1)

Family Consecration to Jesus through Mary

How to Pray the Rosary

1. Make the Sign of the Cross.

   In the name of the Father, and of the Son and of the Holy Spirit. Amen.

2. Holding the Crucifix, say the Apostles' Creed.

   I believe in God, the Father Almighty, Creator of Heaven and earth; and in Jesus Christ, His only Son, Our Lord, who was conceived by the Holy Spirit, born of the Virgin Mary, suffered under Pontius Pilate, was crucified, died, and was buried. He descended into Hell; the third day He rose again from the dead; He ascended into Heaven, and is seated at the right hand of God, the Father almighty; from thence He shall come to judge the living and the dead. I believe in the Holy Spirit, the holy Catholic Church, the communion of saints, the forgiveness of sins, the resurrection of the body, and life everlasting. Amen.

3. On the first bead, say an Our Father.

   Our Father, who art in heaven, hallowed be Thy Name. Thy Kingdom come. Thy Will be done, on earth as it is in Heaven. Give us this day our daily bread. And forgive us our trespasses, as we forgive those who trespass against us. And lead us not into temptation, but deliver us from evil. Amen.

4. Say a Hail Mary on each of the next three beads (you can ask for an increase in the virtues of faith, hope, and charity).

   Hail Mary, full of grace, the Lord is with thee. Blessed art thou among women, and blessed is the fruit of thy womb, Jesus. Holy Mary, Mother of God, pray for us sinners, now and at the hour of our death. Amen.

5. Say the Glory Be.

   Glory be to the Father, and to the Son, and to the Holy Spirit. As it was in the beginning, is now, and ever shall be, world without end. Amen.

6. For each of the five decades, announce the mystery (you can also read a brief reading from Scripture if desired) and say the Our Father.

7. On each of the following ten beads, say a Hail Mary while meditating on the mystery. Then say a Glory Be. Some then say the following prayer requested by the Blessed Virgin Mary at Fatima:

   O my Jesus, forgive us our sins, save us from the fires of hell; lead all souls to Heaven, especially those who have most need of your mercy.

8. After saying the five decades, say the Hail Holy Queen.

   Hail, holy Queen, mother of mercy, our life, our sweetness, and our hope. To thee do we cry, poor banished children of Eve. To thee do we send up our sighs, mourning, and weeping in this valley of tears. Turn then, most gracious advocate, thine eyes of mercy toward us, and after this our exile, show unto us the blessed fruit of thy womb, Jesus. O clement, O loving, O sweet Virgin Mary.

V. Pray for us, O holy Mother of God.
R. That we may be made worthy of the promises of Christ.

Follow the Hail Holy Queen with this dialogue and prayer:

Let us pray: O God, whose Only Begotten Son, by his life, Death, and Resurrection, has purchased for us the rewards of eternal life, grant, we beseech Thee, that while meditating on these mysteries of the most holy Rosary of the Blessed Virgin Mary, we may imitate what they contain and obtain what they promise, through the same Christ our Lord. Amen.

You can say the following if you desire:

Most Sacred Heart of Jesus, have mercy on us.
Immaculate Heart of Mary, pray for us.

9. Conclude the Rosary with the Sign of the Cross.

When the Rosary is said in a group, or, individually prayed before the Blessed Sacrament, you may gain a plenary indulgence under the usual conditions (sacramental Communion, sacramental Confession in the preceding or following eight days, and freedom from all attachment to sin, even venial sin), which includes an Our Father, a Hail Mary, and a Glory Be for the intentions of the Holy Father.

The Divine Mercy Chaplet

The Divine Mercy Chaplet is a special prayer given by Jesus to Saint Faustina Maria Kowalska. It is a powerful prayer to be said for the dying or for any other reason. It is traditionally prayed at 3:00 p.m., which is the Hour of Great Mercy, and it may be prayed using rosary beads.

How to Pray the Divine Mercy Chaplet

1. Make the Sign of the Cross.

   In the name of the Father, and of the Son and of the Holy Spirit. Amen.

2. Say the following opening prayers (optional).

   You expired, Jesus, but the source of life gushed forth for souls, and the ocean of mercy opened up for the whole world. O Fount of Life, unfathomable Divine Mercy, envelop the whole world and empty Yourself out upon us.

   O Blood and Water, which gushed forth from the Heart of Jesus as a fountain of mercy for us, I trust in You! (three times)

3. Say the Our Father.

   Our Father, who art in heaven, hallowed be Thy Name. Thy Kingdom come. Thy Will be done, on earth as it is in Heaven. Give us this day our daily bread. And forgive us our trespasses, as we forgive those who trespass against us. And lead us not into temptation, but deliver us from evil. Amen.

4. Say the Hail Mary.

Hail Mary, full of grace, the Lord is with thee. Blessed art thou among women, and blessed is the fruit of thy womb, Jesus. Holy Mary, Mother of God, pray for us sinners, now and at the hour of our death. Amen.

5. Say the Apostles' Creed.

I believe in God, the Father Almighty, Creator of Heaven and earth; and in Jesus Christ, His only Son, Our Lord, who was conceived by the Holy Spirit, born of the Virgin Mary, suffered under Pontius Pilate, was crucified, died, and was buried. He descended into Hell; the third day He rose again from the dead; He ascended into Heaven, and is seated at the right hand of God, the Father almighty; from thence He shall come to judge the living and the dead. I believe in the Holy Spirit, the holy Catholic Church, the communion of saints, the forgiveness of sins, the resurrection of the body, and life everlasting. Amen.

6. On each "Our Father bead" of a rosary, say the following:

Eternal Father, I offer you the Body and Blood, Soul and Divinity of Your dearly beloved Son, Our Lord, Jesus Christ, in atonement for our sins and those of the whole world.

7. On each "Hail Mary bead," say the following:

   For the sake of His sorrowful Passion, have mercy on us and on the whole world.

8. Repeat for the remaining decades.

9. Conclude by praying the following prayer three times: Holy God, Holy Mighty One, Holy Immortal One, have mercy on us and on the whole world.

10. Say the following closing prayer (optional).

    Eternal God, in whom mercy is endless and the treasury of compassion inexhaustible, look kindly upon us and increase Your mercy in us, that in difficult moments we might not despair nor become despondent, but with great confidence submit ourselves to Your holy will, which is Love and Mercy itself. Amen.

Family Consecration to Jesus through Mary

Marian Prayer of Saint John Henry Newman

O Mother of Jesus, and my Mother, let me dwell with you, cling to you, and love you with ever-increasing love. I promise the honor, love, and trust of a child. Give me a mother's protection, for I need your watchful care. You know better than any other the thoughts and desires of the Sacred Heart. Keep constantly before my mind the same thoughts, the same desires, that my heart may be filled with zeal for the interests of the Sacred Heart of your Divine Son. Instill in me a love of all that is noble, that I may no longer be easily turned to selfishness. Help me, dearest Mother, to acquire the virtues that God wants of me: to forget myself always, to work solely for Him, without fear of sacrifice. I shall always rely on your help to be what Jesus wants me to be. I am His; I am yours, my good Mother! Give me each day your holy and maternal blessing until my last evening on earth, when your Immaculate Heart will present me to the heart of Jesus in heaven, there to love and bless you and your divine Son for all eternity.

Prayer to One's Guardian Angel

Angel of God, my guardian dear, to whom God's love commits me here, ever this day be at my side, to light and guard, to rule and guide. Amen.

Additional Prayers

Prayer to Saint Michael

Saint Michael the Archangel, defend us in battle. Be our defense against the wickedness and snares of the devil. May God rebuke him, we humbly pray, and do thou, O Prince of the heavenly hosts, by the power of God, thrust into hell Satan and all the evil spirits who prowl about the world seeking the ruin of souls. Amen.

Child's Prayer to Mary

Dear Mother of Jesus and my Mother, please be with me throughout each day and night. Teach me to be an obedient child, desiring to come closer and closer to your Son, Jesus, who is our King! Please mold my little heart and soul into what will be most pleasing to your Son, and protect me from anything that will harm my heart and soul. I give my heart to you. Amen.

Family Consecration to Jesus through Mary

Litany of Humility

This popular prayer was composed by Rafael Cardinal Merry de Val, the secretary of state for Pope Saint Pius X in 1963.

O Jesus, meek and humble of heart, *hear me.*
From the desire of being esteemed, *deliver me, O Jesus.*
From the desire of being loved, *deliver me, O Jesus.*
From the desire of being extolled, *deliver me, O Jesus.*
From the desire of being honored, *deliver me, O Jesus.*
From the desire of being praised, *deliver me, O Jesus.*
From the desire of being preferred to others,
 deliver me, O Jesus.
From the desire of being consulted, *deliver me, O Jesus.*
From the desire of being approved, *deliver me, O Jesus.*
From the fear of being humiliated, *deliver me, O Jesus.*
From the fear of being despised, *deliver me, O Jesus.*
From the fear of suffering rebukes, *deliver me, O Jesus.*
From the fear of being calumniated, *deliver me, O Jesus.*
From the fear of being forgotten, *deliver me, O Jesus.*
From the fear of being ridiculed, *deliver me, O Jesus.*
From the fear of being wronged, *deliver me, O Jesus.*
From the fear of being suspected, *deliver me, O Jesus.*
That others may be loved more than I, *Jesus, grant me*
 the grace to desire it.
That others may be esteemed more than I, *Jesus, grant me*
 the grace to desire it.
That, in the opinion of the world, others may increase
 and I may decrease, *Jesus, grant me the grace to desire it.*
That others may be chosen and I set aside, *Jesus, grant me*
 the grace to desire it.
That others may be praised and I go unnoticed, *Jesus, grant*
 me the grace to desire it.

That others may be preferred to me in everything, *Jesus, grant me the grace to desire it.*
That others may become holier than I, provided that I may become as holy as I should, *Jesus, grant me the grace to desire it.*
Amen.

Act of Consecration to the Immaculata
(by Saint Maximilian Mary Kolbe)

Immaculata, Queen of Heaven and earth, refuge of sinners and most loving Mother, to whom God wanted to entrust the entire order of mercy, I prostrate myself before you, poor sinner that I am; I humbly implore you to accept my entire being as your good and your property, and to act within me and in all the faculties of my soul and body, in all my life, death, and eternity, as it will please you. Make of me whatever you will, to accomplish what is written concerning you: "She will crush the serpent's head," and also: "Through you, all the heresies of the world have been overcome."

In your immaculate and most merciful hands, may I be a docile instrument to make you known and loved by many lukewarm or wayward souls, and thus extend the most sacred Reign of Jesus as much as possible.

In truth, only where you come do you obtain the grace of the conversion and sanctification of souls, because all graces flow from the Sacred Heart of Jesus onto us all by passing through your hands.

Family Consecration to Jesus through Mary

Short Daily Consecration Prayer

My Queen and my Mother, I give myself entirely to you;
and to show my devotion to you, I consecrate to you this
day my eyes, my ears, my mouth, my heart, my whole
being without reserve. Wherefore, good Mother, as I am
your own, keep me, guard me, as your property and possession. Amen.

"Totally Yours" Consecration Prayer
(by Saint John Paul II)

Immaculate Conception, Mary, my Mother.
Live in me. Act in me. Speak in and through me.
Think your thoughts in my mind. Love, through my heart.
Give me your dispositions and feelings.
Teach, lead, and guide me to Jesus.
Correct, enlighten, and expand my thoughts and behavior.
Possess my soul. Take over my entire personality and life.
Replace it with yourself.
Incline me to constant adoration and thanksgiving.
Pray in me and through me.
Let me live in you and keep me in this union always. Amen.

Saint Teresa of Calcutta's Consecration Prayer
(prayed daily by the Missionaries of Charity)

My Queen and my Mother, I give You myself and to show my
devotion to you I consecrate to you this day, and for ever, my
eyes, ears, mouth, heart, wholly and without reserve. Wherefore good Mother as I am your own, keep me, defend me, as
your property and your own possession. Amen.

Additional Prayers

Fatima Prayers

Pardon Prayer

The Angel of Peace taught this prayer to the three shepherd children during his first apparition, in 1916.

My God, I believe, I adore, I hope, and I love You! I beg pardon for those who do not believe, do not adore, do not hope, and do not love You.

Angel's Prayer

During his third apparition in 1916 to the shepherd children, while the Blessed Sacrament was suspended in the air, the Angel of Peace prostrated himself and prayed this prayer.

O Most Holy Trinity, Father, Son, and Holy Spirit, I adore You profoundly. I offer You the most precious Body, Blood, Soul, and Divinity of Jesus Christ, present in all the tabernacles of the world, in reparation for the outrages, sacrileges, and indifferences by which He is offended. By the infinite merits of the Sacred Heart of Jesus and the Immaculate Heart of Mary, I beg the conversion of poor sinners.

Eucharistic Prayer

During the apparition of May 13, 1917, this prayer was communicated to the three shepherd children by an interior impulse.

Most Holy Trinity, I adore You! My God, my God, I love You in the Most Blessed Sacrament!

Family Consecration to Jesus through Mary

Sacrifice Prayer

During the July 13, 1917, apparition, Our Lady of Fatima taught this prayer to the children to be prayed whenever they made a sacrifice to God.

O Jesus, it is for love of You, for the conversion of sinners, and in reparation for the sins committed against the Immaculate Heart of Mary.

Decade Prayer

During the July 13, 1917, apparition, Our Lady of Fatima requested that this prayer be prayed after each decade of the Rosary.

O my Jesus, forgive us our sins, save us from the fires of hell; lead all souls to Heaven, especially those who have most need of Your mercy.

Divine Praises

It is always fitting to praise God. As well, Mary Most Holy is included in the Divine Praises. It is a beautiful and powerful prayer.

Blessed be God.

Blessed be his Holy Name.

Blessed be Jesus Christ, true God and true man.

Blessed be the name of Jesus.

Blessed be His Most Sacred Heart

Blessed be His Most Precious Blood.

Blessed be Jesus in the Most Holy Sacrament of the Altar.

Blessed be the Holy Spirit, the Paraclete

Blessed be the great Mother of God, Mary Most Holy.

Blessed be her holy and Immaculate Conception.

Blessed be her glorious Assumption.

Blessed be the name of Mary, Virgin and Mother.

Blessed be Saint Joseph, her most chaste spouse.

Blessed be God in His angels and in His saints.

Litany of Saint Joseph

Lord, have mercy on us.

Christ, have mercy on us.

Lord, have mercy on us. Christ, hear us.

Christ, graciously hear us.

God the Father of Heaven, *have mercy on us.*

God the Son, Redeemer of the world, *have mercy on us.*

God the Holy Spirit, *have mercy on us.*

Holy Trinity, one God, *have mercy on us.*

Holy Mary, *pray for us.*

Saint Joseph, *pray for us.*

Illustrious son of David, *pray for us.*

Light of the patriarchs, *pray for us.*

Family Consecration to Jesus through Mary

Spouse of the Mother of God, *pray for us.*

Chaste guardian of the Virgin, *pray for us.*

Foster father of the Son of God, *pray for us.*

Watchful defender of Christ, *pray for us.*

Head of the Holy Family, *pray for us.*

Joseph most just, *pray for us.*

Joseph most chaste, *pray for us.*

Joseph most prudent, *pray for us.*

Joseph most valiant, *pray for us.*

Joseph most obedient, *pray for us.*

Joseph most faithful, *pray for us.*

Mirror of patience, *pray for us.*

Lover of poverty, *pray for us.*

Model of workmen, *pray for us.*

Glory of domestic life, *pray for us.*

Guardian of virgins, *pray for us.*

Pillar of families, *pray for us.*

Solace of the afflicted, *pray for us.*

Hope of the sick, *pray for us.*

Patron of the dying, *pray for us.*

Terror of demons, *pray for us.*

Protector of Holy Church, *pray for us.*

Lamb of God, who takest away the sins of the world,
   spare us, O Lord.

Lamb of God, who takest away the sins of the world,
   graciously hear us, O Lord.

Lamb of God, who takest away the sins of the world,
   have mercy on us.

Additional Prayers

Memorare

Remember, O most gracious Virgin Mary, that never
was it known that anyone who fled to thy protection,
implored thy help, or sought thine intercession was left
unaided. Inspired by this confidence, I fly unto thee, O
Virgin of virgins, my mother; to thee do I come, before
thee I stand, sinful and sorrowful. O Mother of the Word
Incarnate, despise not my petitions, but in thy mercy hear
and answer me. Amen.

Memorare to Saint Joseph

Remember, O most chaste spouse of the Virgin Mary, that
never was it known that anyone who implored your help
and sought your intercession were left unassisted. Full
of confidence in your power, I fly unto you and beg your
protection. Despise not, O Guardian of the Redeemer, my
humble supplication, but in your bounty, hear and answer
me. Amen.

Prayer of Saint Augustine

O Jesus Christ, You are my Father, my merciful God, my
great king, my good shepherd, my only master, my best
helper, my beloved friend of overwhelming beauty, my
living bread, my eternal priest. You are my guide to my
heavenly home, my one true light, my holy joy, my true
way, my shining wisdom, my unfeigned simplicity, the
peace and harmony of my soul, my perfect safeguard, my
bounteous inheritance, my everlasting salvation.

My loving Lord, Jesus Christ, why have I ever loved or
desired anything else in my life but You, my God? Where
was I when I was not in communion with You? From now

on, I direct all my desires to be inspired by You and cen-
tered on You. I direct them to press forward, for they have
tarried long enough, to hasten toward their goal, to seek
the One they yearn for.

O Jesus, let him who does not love you be accursed
and filled with bitterness. O gentle Jesus, let every worthy feeling of mine show You love, take delight in You,
and admire You. O God of my heart and my inheritance,
Christ Jesus, may my heart mellow before the influence
of Your spirit, and may You live in me. May the flame of
Your love burn in my soul. May it burn incessantly on
the altar of my heart. May it glow in my innermost being.
May it spread its heat into the hidden recesses of my soul,
and on the day of my consummation, may I appear before
You consumed in Your love. Amen.

Appendix D

Marian Devotions and Resources

Marian Saturdays

The Church teaches that Saturday is a special day for the holy Mother of God. We can honor Mary in a more fervent way each Saturday. Specifically, the Church states:

> Saturdays stand out among those days dedicated to the Virgin Mary. These are designated as *memorials of the Blessed Virgin Mary* (218). This memorial derives from carolingian time (ninth century), but the reasons for having chosen Saturday for its observance are unknown (219). While many explanations have been advanced to explain this choice, none is completely satisfactory from the point of view of the history of popular piety (220).
>
> Prescinding from its historical origins, today the memorial rightly emphasizes certain values "to which contemporary spirituality is more sensitive: it is a remembrance of the maternal example and discipleship of the Blessed Virgin Mary who, strengthened by faith and hope, on that great Saturday on which Our Lord lay in the tomb, was the only one of the disciples to hold vigil in expectation of the Lord's

resurrection; it is a prelude and introduction to the celebration of Sunday, the weekly memorial of the Resurrection of Christ; it is a sign that the "Virgin Mary is continuously present and operative in the life of the Church" (221).

Popular piety is also sensitive to the Saturday memorial of the Blessed Virgin Mary. The statutes of many religious communities and associations of the faithful prescribe that special devotion be paid to the Holy Mother of God on Saturdays, sometimes through specified pious exercises composed precisely for Saturdays (222).[88]

Consider making your Saturdays more meaningful by making them more Marian! Perhaps you can offer special prayers of reparation to the Blessed Mother.

Five First Saturdays Devotion

I would like to give a bit of a background on the important Five First Saturdays devotion requested by the Blessed Mother to hopefully inspire you to carry it out as often as you can. This devotion came about through a message that Our Lady of Fatima (the Blessed Mother) gave when appearing to three shepherd children in Fatima, Portugal. They were Sister Lucia dos Santos and her cousins Saint Francisco Marto and his little sister Saint Jacinta Marto. The two youngest visionaries were canonized in 2017. The cause for canonization has been opened for Sister Lucia, who lived until she was

---

[88] Congregation for Divine Worship and for the Discipline of the Sacraments, *Directory on Popular Piety and the Liturgy: Principles and Guidelines* (December 2001), no. 188, http://www.vatican.va/roman_curia/congregations/ccdds/documents/rc_con_ccdds_doc_20020513_vers-direttorio_en.html#Chapter%20Five.

almost ninety-eight years old. Since Sister Lucia lived so long, it will take an extensive time for the Church to investigate her life and virtue fully.

Our Lady of Fatima requested of the faithful that they pray in a certain way on the first Saturday of five consecutive months, in order to make up for the five types of offenses committed against the Blessed Mother's Immaculate Heart. Jesus revealed to Sister Lucia the offenses and blasphemies. He said:

> Daughter, the motive is simple. There are five kinds of offenses and blasphemies spoken against the Immaculate Heart of Mary: blasphemies: (1) against her Immaculate Conception; (2) against her perpetual virginity; (3) against her divine maternity, refusing at the same time to accept her as the Mother of mankind; (4) by those who try publicly to implant in the hearts of children an indifference, contempt, and even hate for this Immaculate Mother; and (5) for those who insult her directly in her sacred images.[89]

Our Lady of Fatima promised that by praying this way, world problems could be avoided and sinners could be converted. Unfortunately, this devotion is considered the most forgotten part of the Fatima message.

When Sister Lucia was a postulant in the Congregation of the Dorothean Sisters in Pontevedra, Spain, Father P. Aparicio, S.J., her spiritual director, requested that Sister Lucia write down the details of the apparitions, but to do so in the third person. Sister Lucia describes the first apparition at Pontevedra, Spain in this way:

---

[89] World Apostolate of Fatima, *Spiritual Guide for the Salvation of Souls and World Peace* (Washington, NJ: World Apostolate of Fatima, 2008), 128–129.

On December 10, 1925, the most holy Virgin appeared to her, and by her side, elevated on a luminous cloud, was [the Christ] child. The most holy Virgin rested her hand on [Sister Lucia's] shoulder, and as she did so, she showed her a heart encircled in thorns, which she was holding in her other hand. At the same time, the [Christ] Child said: "Have compassion on the Heart of your most holy Mother, covered with thorns, with which ungrateful men pierce it at every moment, and there is no one to make an act of reparation to remove them." Then the most holy Virgin said: "Look, my daughter, at my Heart, surrounded with thorns with which ungrateful men pierce me at every moment by their blasphemies and ingratitude. You at least try to console me and say that I promise to assist at the hour of death, with the graces necessary for salvation, all those who, on the first Saturday of five consecutive months, shall confess [their sins], receive Holy Communion, recite five decades of the Rosary, and keeping me company for fifteen minutes while meditating on the fifteen mysteries of the Rosary, with the intention of making reparation to me."[90]

Making the Five First Saturdays Devotion

The necessary components of the practice of the Five First Saturday Devotion, otherwise known as "Communions of Reparation," make reparation to the Immaculate Heart for the five offenses, are these:

1. Go to Confession (within eight days before or after the first Saturday).
2. Receive Holy Communion on the first Saturday.

[90] Lucia dos Santos, *Fatima in Lucia's Own Words: Sister Lucia's Memoirs*, ed. Louis Kondor, S.V.D., trans. Dominican Nuns of Perpetual Rosary (N.p.: Fatima Postulation Center, 1976), 195.

3. Pray five decades of the Rosary.
4. Keep Our Lady company for fifteen minutes while meditating on the mysteries of the Rosary.

The Brown Scapular

Many devotees of Mother Mary wear her Brown Scapular. Marian piety includes "devotion" to various scapulars, with the Scapular of Our Lady of Mount Carmel being the most common, recommended by the Magisterium throughout history. The Scapular of Mount Carmel, otherwise known as the Brown Scapular, is a much smaller version of the religious habit of the Order of the Friars of the Blessed Virgin of Mount Carmel.

The Congregation for Divine Worship and for the Discipline of the Sacraments instructs, "The Scapular is an external sign of the filial relationship established between the Blessed Virgin Mary, Mother and Queen of Mount Carmel, and the faithful who entrust themselves totally to her protection, who have recourse to her maternal intercession, who are mindful of the primacy of the spiritual life and the need for prayer."[91]

There are other scapulars as well, such as the Blue Scapular, which is promoted by the Confraternity of the Immaculate Conception of the Most Blessed Virgin Mary (with the Congregation of Marian Fathers). According to its website, the confraternity "has existed since the 18th century to promote the devotion to the Immaculate Conception of our Immaculate Mother so her motherly

---

[91] Congregation for Divine Worship and for the Discipline of the Sacraments, *Directory on Popular Piety*, no. 205. See *The Doctrinal Statement on the Brown Scapular of Our Lady of Mount Carmel*, which includes the "Rite of Blessing of and Enrollment in the Scapular of the Blessed Virgin Mary of Mount Carmel," http://dev.thereseocds. org/wp-content/uploads/2017/04/Scapular-Catechesis-Online.pdf.

love might strengthen, comfort, and fill hearts with joy, the source of which is her Son, Jesus Christ, our Savior. The external sign of belonging to the Confraternity is the Blue Scapular."

National Shrine of The Divine Mercy
Eden Hill
Stockbridge, MA 01263
(800) 462-7426
https://www.marian.org/confraternity/

The Miraculous Medal

The Miraculous Medal is a popular sacramental. The Congregation for Divine Worship and for the Discipline of the Sacraments tells us, "The faithful like to wear medals bearing effigies of the Blessed Virgin Mary. These are a witness of faith and a sign of veneration of the Holy Mother of God, as well as of trust in her maternal protection." The Church blesses such Marian objects of devotion because "they help to remind the faithful of the love of God, and to increase trust in the Blessed Virgin Mary" (258).

The Miraculous Medal originated in 1830 when Our Lady appeared to Saint Catherine Labouré and instructed her to construct the medal according to the description she gave her, which "recalls the mystery of Redemption, the love of the Sacred Heart of Jesus and of the Sorrowful Heart of Mary. It signifies the mediatory role of the Blessed Virgin Mary, the mystery of the Church, the relationship between Heaven and earth, this life and eternal life." Saints such as Maximillian Kolbe and Teresa of Calcutta have widely distributed the medal. The Church instructs, "The Miraculous Medal is never to be regarded as a talisman or lead to any form of blind credulity (260). The promise of Our Lady that 'those who were the medal will receive great graces,' requires a humble and tenacious commitment to the Christian message, faithful and persevering prayer, and a good Christian life."[92]

Prayer to Our Lady of the Miraculous Medal

O Virgin Mother of God, Mary immaculate, we dedicate and consecrate ourselves to you under the title of Our Lady of the Miraculous Medal.

May this medal be for each one of us a sure sign of your affection for us and a constant reminder of our duties toward you. Ever while wearing it, may we be blessed by your loving protection and preserved in the grace of your Son.

O most powerful Virgin, Mother of our Savior, keep us close to you every moment of our lives. Obtain for us, your children, the grace of a happy death; so that, in union with you, we may enjoy the bliss of heaven forever. Amen.

O Mary, conceived without sin, pray for us who have recourse to you. (three times)

Marian Associations

Militia of the Immaculata, USA (MI)

MI is a worldwide evangelization movement founded by Saint Maximilian Kolbe in 1917 that encourages total consecration to the Blessed Virgin Mary as a means of spiritual renewal for individuals and society.

---

[92] Congregation for Divine Worship and for the Discipline of the Sacraments, *Directory on Popular Piety*, no. 206.

Family Consecration to Jesus through Mary

MI National-USA
P.O. Box 5547, Peoria, IL 61601
https://missionimmaculata.com

Central Association of the Miraculous Medal

From the website: "The Central Association of the Miraculous Medal is dedicated to spreading devotion to Mary Immaculate and her Miraculous Medal, supporting the promotion of this devotion, helping the formation and education of seminarians, providing care to the aged and infirm Priests and Brothers of the Eastern Province, and supporting programs that provide assistance to the poor."

Central Association of the Miraculous Medal
475 E. Chelten Avenue, Philadelphia, PA 19144
https://cammonline.org/who-we-are/

Association of the Miraculous Medal

From the website: "The Association of the Miraculous Medal brings Jesus Christ to the world by inspiring devotion to Mary, Our Lady of the Miraculous Medal, through whom we unite ourselves in prayer to grow in holiness while supporting the apostolic mission and charitable work of our Vincentian priests and brothers."

Association of the Miraculous Medal
1811 West Saint Joseph Street, Perryville, Missouri, 63775
https://www.amm.org/AboutAMM/Our%20Mission.aspx

Chaplet of the Ten Evangelical
Virtues of the Mother of God

This chaplet helps us to reflect on Mary's virtues and invoke her powerful, maternal intercession. It may be prayed on a chaplet of ten beads or on ten beads of a rosary.[93]

Br. Andrew R. Maczynski, MIC, said, "Whoever wants to glorify the Blessed Virgin Mary and wishes to stay under her protection, should love and respect her — but, above all, should exercise the evangelical virtues and, through this, shall follow Mary's example."[94]

1. Make the Sign of the Cross.
2. Pray one Our Father.
3. Pray a Hail Mary for each of the ten virtues below. After the words "Holy Mary, Mother of God," recite the virtue and continue with the prayer. For example, "Holy Mary, Mother of God most pure, pray for us sinners, now and at the hour of our death. Amen."

   Virtues:
   Most pure (Matt. 1:18, 20, 23; Luke 1:24, 34)
   Most prudent (Luke 2:19, 51)
   Most humble (Luke 1:48)
   Most faithful (Luke 1:45; John 2:5)
   Most devout (Luke 1:46–47; Acts 1:14)
   Most obedient (Luke 1:38; 2:21–22, 27)
   Most poor (Luke 2:7)

---

[93] Additional details about this devotion can be found on website of the Marians of the Immaculate Conception, https://padrimariani. org/en/r_pray_virtues/#chaplet.

[94] Br. Andrew R. Maczynski, MIC, "Chaplet of the Ten Virtues of the Blessed Virgin Mary: A Powerful Prayer That Can Help You Reflect on Mary's Virtues and Imitate Her," Marians of the Immaculate Conception, https://www.marian.org/mary/prayers/chaplet.php.

Family Consecration to Jesus through Mary

> Most patient (John 19:25)
> Most merciful (Luke 1:39, 56)
> Most sorrowful (Luke 2:35)

V. Glory be to the Father and to the Son and to the Holy Spirit.

R. As it was in the beginning, is now, and ever shall be, world without end. Amen

V. In your conception, O Virgin Mary, you were immaculate.

R. Pray for us to God our Father, whose Son, Jesus Christ, you brought forth into the world.

Let us pray: Omnipotent Father, You prepared the Virgin Mary to be the worthy Mother of Your Son. You let her share beforehand in the salvation Jesus Christ would bring by His death, Resurrection, and Ascension and kept her sinless from the first moment of her conception. Help us by her prayers to live in Your presence without sin. We ask this in the Name of Jesus Christ our Lord, in unity with the Holy Spirit. Amen.

V. The Virgin Mary's Immaculate Conception

R. Be our health and our protection. Amen

Acknowledgments

I am deeply grateful to my parents, Eugene Joseph and Alexandra Mary Cooper, for bringing me into the world and raising me in a large Catholic family, and to my grandmother Alexandra Mary Uzwiak for setting a beautiful prayerful example. To my brothers and sisters — Alice Jean, Gene, Gary, Barbara, Tim, Michael, and David — thank you for being a wonderful part of my life.

My heartfelt loving gratitude goes to my husband, Dave, and my beloved children — Justin, Chaldea, Jessica, Joseph, and Mary-Catherine — for their continued love and support, and to my precious grandsons, Shepherd and Leo. I love you all dearly!

I am grateful to my friend Servant of God Father John Hardon, S.J., who spiritually directed and encouraged me and is no doubt continuing from Heaven! Also, an exuberant thank-you to dear Mother Teresa for playing a huge role in shaping me spiritually, which I know she continues even now, and to Father Andrew Apostoli, CFR, a dear friend and spiritual director, now helping me from Heaven!

I owe very special thanks to Sophia Institute Press, to Charlie McKinney, and to John Barger, and the wonderful team at Sophia Institute Press who helped get this book out to you!

Family Consecration to Jesus through Mary

Finally, I am extremely thankful for my readership, viewership, and listenership, and to all those I meet in my travels. I pray for you every day. Thank you for being part of my fascinating journey through life! Please pray for me too. Stay close to Jesus and Mary! May God bless you in great abundance!

About the Author

Known the world over, Donna-Marie Cooper O'Boyle is a Catholic wife, the mother of five children, a grandmother, and an award-winning and best-selling author and journalist, television host, international speaker, and pilgrimage and retreat leader. She is the television host of EWTN's *Everyday Blessings for Catholic Moms*, *Catholic Mom's Cafe*, and *Feeding Your Family's Soul*, which she created to teach, encourage, and inspire Catholic families. Her love for children prompted her to teach catechism, which she has done for almost thirty years. Donna-Marie serves as an extraordinary Eucharistic minister in her parish and was noted as one of the "Top Ten Most Fascinating Catholics" in 2009 by *Faith and Family Live*. She was blessed with a decade-long friendship with Saint Teresa of Calcutta, became a Lay Missionary of Charity, and started a branch of the Lay Missionaries of Charity. For many years, Donna-Marie's spiritual director was Servant of God John A. Hardon, S.J., who also served as one of Mother Teresa's spiritual directors.

Donna-Marie was invited by the Holy See in 2008 to participate in an international congress for women at the Vatican to mark the twentieth anniversary of the apostolic letter *Mulieris Dignitatem*

(*On the Dignity and Vocation of Women*). She received apostolic blessings from Saint John Paul II and Pope Benedict XVI on her books and work and a special blessing from Saint John Paul II for her work with Saint Teresa of Calcutta. Donna-Marie has received many awards for her books and work, including awards from the Catholic Press Association, Connecticut Press Club, the National Federation of Press Women, and a Media Award from the American Cancer Society for her column.

Donna-Marie is the author of more than thirty books on faith and family, some of which have been translated into other languages as well as in braille. Her memoir is *The Kiss of Jesus: How Mother Teresa and the Saints Helped Me to Discover the Beauty of the Cross*. Donna-Marie's work has been featured in several Catholic magazines and national newspapers, on several websites, and in Internet columns. Some of her articles have been featured in *L'Osservatore Romano, Magnificat* magazine, *National Catholic Register, Catholic World Report, Our Sunday Visitor Newsweekly*, and in other periodicals.

She has been profiled on many television shows, including Fox News, *Rome Reports, Vatican Insider, Women of Grace, Sunday Night Prime, EWTN Live, The Choices We Face, At Home with Jim and Joy, The Journey Home*, and *Faith & Culture* on EWTN. She is a regular guest on many national radio shows as well and has hosted her own show.

Donna-Marie lives with her family in beautiful rural New England, admiring God's creation. She lectures throughout the world on topics relating to Catholic and Christian women, faith, families, Our Lady of Fatima, the saints and angels, and her friend Mother Teresa. She can be reached at her websites, donnacooperoboyle.com and feedingyourfamilyssoul.com, where you can learn more about Donna-Marie's books, ministry, and pilgrimages and where she also maintains blogs.

Sophia Institute

Sophia Institute is a nonprofit institution that seeks to nurture the spiritual, moral, and cultural life of souls and to spread the Gospel of Christ in conformity with the authentic teachings of the Roman Catholic Church.

Sophia Institute Press fulfills this mission by offering translations, reprints, and new publications that afford readers a rich source of the enduring wisdom of mankind.

Sophia Institute also operates the popular online resource CatholicExchange.com. *Catholic Exchange* provides world news from a Catholic perspective as well as daily devotionals and articles that will help readers to grow in holiness and live a life consistent with the teachings of the Church.

In 2013, Sophia Institute launched Sophia Institute for Teachers to renew and rebuild Catholic culture through service to Catholic education. With the goal of nurturing the spiritual, moral, and cultural life of souls, and an abiding respect for the role and work of teachers, we strive to provide materials and programs that are at once enlightening to the mind and ennobling to the heart; faithful and complete, as well as useful and practical.

Sophia Institute gratefully recognizes the Solidarity Association for preserving and encouraging the growth of our apostolate over the course of many years. Without their generous and timely support, this book would not be in your hands.

www.SophiaInstitute.com
www.CatholicExchange.com
www.SophiaInstituteforTeachers.org

Sophia Institute Press® is a registered trademark of Sophia Institute.
Sophia Institute is a tax-exempt institution as defined by the
Internal Revenue Code, Section 501(c)(3). Tax ID 22-2548708.